T0054154

Praise for *Guiding the N*

"This powerful text serves as a road map to help guide the next generation toward current and future successes. Using relevant stories, proven models, and practical strategies, Jonathan Catherman offers the reader an opportunity to navigate the challenges faced in harnessing the unlimited potential of our teens. Moving beyond the traditional and often outdated notions of leadership, *Guiding the Next Great Generation* is a must-read to help inform and empower teachers, coaches, stakeholders, and parents to use strengths, stewardship, and purpose as catalysts to help guide and develop future leaders. This text will now be an integral part of our teaching and learning curriculum for years to come."

Matthew Ohlson, PhD, director of the Taylor Leadership Institute and associate professor in the Department of Leadership, School Counseling & Sport Management, University of North Florida

"We have no choice about aging, but getting old is a decision all humans make. Reading *Guiding the Next Great Generation*, I felt like a student and a teacher. Jonathan has created a must-read guide for generations of leaders."

Ron Kitchens, CEO of Southwest Michigan First and author of *Uniquely You: Transform Your Organization by Becoming the Leader Only You Can Be*

"Jonathan Catherman presents a compelling case about the potential for today's youth to become the next great generation. With chapter after chapter filled with practical tools and insights, this book is a must-read for parents, teachers, and coaches, as well as any adult who is in a position to support, guide, and positively influence young individuals, helping them discover how to live a life of service and purpose. After reading *Guiding the Next Great Generation*, you'll be inspired to do even more to equip young people in your life with the skills needed to solve the challenges of tomorrow and prepare them for greatness."

Nicole Suydam, president and CEO of
Goodwill of Orange County, CA

Praise for *The Manual to Manhood*

"Consider this your survival guide on the sometimes rocky road to becoming a man. You're going to love this book!"

Dr. Les Parrott, author of *The Parent You Want to Be*

"*The Manual to Manhood* is an engaging, fun, and insightful how-to guide for guys on how to become a man. For those who want to build self-confidence, become independent, and fulfill your full potential, this book is for you."

Sean Covey, author of the international bestseller
The 7 Habits of Highly Effective Teens

"Every guy needs to know how to do everything in *The Manual to Manhood*. Jonathan is offering 'young men in the making' the truth about commonsense, real-world ways to gaining respect and avoid embarrassment on the challenging road to manhood. Every young man should read this book!"

Rick Johnson, bestselling author of *Better Dads,
Stronger Sons* and *A Man in the Making*

"*The Manual to Manhood* is the perfect book for parents, teachers, coaches, and mentors looking to help boys learn valuable life lessons, develop strengths, and discover their unique identity on the journey to manhood."

Matthew Ohlson, PhD, College of Education, University
of Florida, education and school improvement consultant,
and proud father of three sons

RAISING
THEM
READY

RAISING THEM READY

Practical Ways to Prepare Your Kids for Life on Their Own

Jonathan and Erica Catherman

Revell

a division of Baker Publishing Group
Grand Rapids, Michigan

Published by Revell
a division of Baker Publishing Group
PO Box 6287, Grand Rapids, MI 49516-6287
www.revellbooks.com

Printed in the United States of America

Library of Congress Cataloging-in-Publication Data
Names: Catherman, Jonathan, author. | Catherman, Erica, 1975– author.
Title: Raising them ready : practical ways to prepare your kids for life on their own / Jonathan and Erica Catherman.
Description: Grand Rapids, MI : Revell, a division of Baker Publishing Group, [2022]
Identifiers: LCCN 2021042941 | ISBN 9780800736583 (paperback) | ISBN 9780800741433 (casebound) | ISBN 9781493428908 (ebook)
Subjects: LCSH: Young adults—Conduct of life. | Teenagers—Conduct of life. | Young adults—Life skills guides. | Teenagers—Life skills guides. | Parent and teenager.
Classification: LCC HQ796 .C394 2022 | DDC 305.235—dc23
LC record available at https://lccn.loc.gov/2021042941

Scripture quotations labeled MSG are taken from THE MESSAGE, copyright © 1993, 2002, 2018 by Eugene H. Peterson. Used by permission of NavPress. All rights reserved. Represented by Tyndale House Publishers, Inc.

Published in association with the Books & Such Literary Agency, 52 Mission Circle, Suite 122, PMB 170, Santa Rosa, CA, 95409-5370, www.booksandsuch.com

Some names and details have been changed to protect the privacy of the individuals involved.

All emojis designed by OpenMoji—the open-source emoji and icon project. License: CC BY-SA 4.0

Baker Publishing Group publications use paper produced from sustainable forestry practices and post-consumer waste whenever possible.

22   23   24   25   26   27   28   7   6   5   4   3   2   1

CONTENTS

INTRODUCTION

You know what they say: "There's a first time for everything." Have you ever noticed we hear these words only when someone is trying to make an uncertain situation feel a little more comfortable? Maybe that's why every loving mother and father has taken a deep breath and whispered to themselves in their most self-assuring tone, *There's a first time for everything*, while facing two uncertain parenting firsts. Their first day home alone with a newborn baby and the first day home alone after their baby is all grown up and sets out on their own.

Both days arrive packed with great anticipation and more than a few questions. Looking down at their sleeping child snugly wrapped in a blanket like a baby burrito, the magnitude of their infant's fragility leaves many parents awash in a mix of emotions. One minute they are overcome with joy and the next, anxiety. On that first day home alone, it's completely understandable for parents to quietly ask themselves, "Are we really ready for this?" Years later, a similar question creeps into the thoughts of even the most seasoned parents. As they watch their grown child pack up, wave goodbye, and set out on their own, it's totally normal for parents to wonder out loud, "Are they really ready for this?"

When the years between their first day home and first day away go as hoped, we know a remarkable transformation has occurred in the lives of our children. Once small and dependent on their parents for everything, our kids somehow survive the diaper rashes, home haircuts, bike crashes, and puberty to miraculously grow up to become happy, healthy, independent adults. Or so we've hoped.

Let's just say it now and get it out in the open early. Being a parent is difficult. Actually, let's be more specific. Being a consistent, patient, engaging, accessible, responsive, rational, present, safe, and loving parent who raises their children to become confident, capable, and kind young adults—now that's difficult.

When by the grace of God we manage to guide our kids down the road between childhood and adulthood in a way that releases them into the world relatively unscathed, then you'd think we could relax. But we won't really. Not all the way, that is. Because though our parenting responsibilities fade over time, we'll always be there for our children as they face life's many demands.

From personal experience, most parents have a pretty good idea of what's on the long list of demands their kids will face while growing up. Then there's all the new stuff our kids are dealing with that didn't even exist when we were young. This means raising kids right in our rapidly changing world includes raising them *ready* to take on the types of challenges and threats that we didn't know about when we were their age.

So, what does it mean to raise kids ready today? To many parents, "ready" sounds like a titanic task. Ready for what? Half the time our kids feel blindsided by stuff they never saw coming. Resilient as we know kids can be, the demands of our world can easily inflict great damage on the hulls of their fragile minds, hearts, spirits, and bodies. From internet trolls and online bullies to a global pandemic and political unrest. Social injustice, racial inequity, academic pressure, the burden of stress, boredom, and the always-in-their-face comparison of their life to the perfectly staged #bestlife of online "influencers" can leave many kids feeling confused and less than important. How do we safely and successfully help our children navigate through the stages of their young lives when we know such great and often damaging forces lie in wait?

There is no easy answer to this very real, very difficult parenting predicament. Yet, there is one thing we know for certain about raising children who grow into confident, capable, and kind adults. Those who are taught to take care of the seemingly little things in childhood are more prepared to steward the much larger opportunities and responsibilities of adulthood.

We became first-time parents in early 2001. We doubled down three years later with the addition of a second child to our young, ambitious family. In the two decades since, more than a few things have become crystal clear to us as parents. Mostly through trial and error. Here are our top ten favorite lessons learned in the years between our kids' first day home and their leaving home to launch into life on their own.

10. Potty training a child and a puppy at the same time is extremely poor planning.

9. Kids desperately want to see and be seen, to hear and be heard, to know and be known, and to love and be loved.

8. Family needs to be the kindest people and home the safest place on the planet.

7. There is no accurate calculation for converting the distance between highway rest stops to the maximum volume of a ten-year-old's Gatorade-flooded bladder.

6. The absolute worst measures of a child's value are mirrors, "likes," grades, and trophies.

5. Attempting to revive the glory days by living vicariously through our kids is a recipe for disaster.

4. Cell phones and high-speed Wi-Fi access are privileges we share with our children and are not to be confused with their inalienable rights.

3. There is nothing in the world our kids can do to make us love them any less.

2. Not liking what our teenager is doing is not the same as not loving them.

1. Their greatness tomorrow begins with our guidance today.

The truth is, we have racked up more well-earned parenting lessons over the years than can possibly be counted. It's probably safest to sum them all up in the understanding that when it comes to learning about parenting, reading books can help, but nothing beats real-life experience. Looking at our own adventures in parenting, we feel the need to say we are not writing this book in hopes of releasing a new set of child-rearing practices or from the need to share our version of perfect parenting. That would be an impossible task, because as we all know, there is no such thing as perfect parents. Just real ones.

There is also no shortage of books on the topic of raising kids. Our office shelves and side tables are stacked with examples. Familiar cover titles include raising children who are kind, cooperative, gifted, whole, grateful, strong, organized, loving, smart, caring, good, and better kids. Authors range from PhDs, presenting five hundred pages of peer-reviewed academic research, to the been-there, survived-that alpha parent with a legion of loyal roaring followers.

Today's selection of *how to be a better parent* publications could pack a brick-and-mortar library's shelves as tight as sardines in a can. In our experience many of these books sit on one of two shelves: Some are so thick and meaty, readers quickly get the feeling they have bitten off more than they can chew. Others are spread so candy-shell thin, they struggle to offer parents any actual child-rearing nutritional value.

We have chosen to present you with a book that is written for the parents who are doing the best they know how to raise their kids. This includes all types of kids and all types of parents.

Thankfully most people's awareness and understanding of the broad spectrum of kids' learning, behavior, and physical abilities is greater today than ever before. So is our inclusion of the wide-ranging diversity of who is committed to the caregiving. To the biological parents, adoptive parents, foster parents, grandparents parenting their kid's kids, aunts and uncles, and anyone who has taken on the role of "parenting" in a child's life, we are writing for you. You will know how to navigate the chapters to come and how they apply to your unique family. To your kids. No matter the circumstances.

Perhaps you are young and excited to learn everything possible about guiding your precious jewel in ways that foster a balance between developmental science and the harmony of whole child wellness. Or you might be completely exhausted. Clinging to what remains of your fragile sanity, you're skimming pages in search of any nugget of practical advice. Our first goal in the chapters to come is to connect with both the fresh-feeling parents and those admittedly frustrated and beyond fatigued. We hope to relate with you in both a personal and scientifically sound way that is easily understood and relevant to you. By simply and practically discussing what "raising them ready" means in today's hyper-aware, digital drenched, mid-twenty-first-century life, we believe you will discover some helpful parenting insights you can use today. To do this we have divided the book into three unique and equally valuable parts. We have titled them READY, SET, and GO.

Part 1: READY In READY we clarify the multiple aspects of what it *means* to grow up and become an adult, and why some young people are ready for the challenge while others feel threatened by the demands. We'll look into why babies really should come with instructions and what secret to future success your callow (inexperienced and immature) kids share in common with seasoned first responders, professional athletes, and Navy SEALs.

Part 2: SET In SET we discuss the specific mindsets, skillsets, and toolsets that prepare kids to thrive in the years ahead rather than struggle to survive through the unavoidable demands of adulting. You'll have a chance to rate your child's skill levels and assess how able they are for their age, and we will provide you with a Launch List of over three hundred combined skills and tools that your kid will benefit from possessing. You may even get some good ideas for their future birthday, holiday, and graduation gifts.

Part 3: GO In GO we encourage you with ways to teach your kids how to become independent in phases by making a Release Plan that includes three stages of letting them go, a little at a time, over time. A plan that values and celebrates your child as they put into practice all you have taught them through Instruction, Guidance, and Counsel.

Like you, we too are still practicing how to be better parents. By practicing, we mean we are dedicated to improving the quality of the soft skills and hard decisions required of us daily as parents. Thankfully, no one mistakenly led us to believe that guiding our kids through their young lives would be easy. If they had, we would feel like epic failures. Instead, we know parenting is a healthy mix of good times and bad moments. Some days we get to claim and celebrate small parenting victories. When we discover something that works in our home, we commit to repeating that behavior as often as possible. Other days we see clearly what isn't working and change our ways. Most of the time we are daily witnesses to the incremental gains our kids make in developing the character and abilities they need to experience both purpose and success. In a way, we are doing our best to work together today so we can successfully live apart from them tomorrow. We know that, for as much as we love our kids and desire for them to remain close, they are not meant to stay home for long. They grow up, mature, and set out to make a life for

14

themselves. On their own. It's our job as parents to prepare them the best we know how.

It helps that in addition to being a husband and father, I (Jonathan) am a sociologist. Over the past three decades I've dedicated my career to researching, writing, and consulting on the shifts in generational norms and about life skills and personal character development in youth. The greatest personal and professional blessing in my life is to be best friends and true partners with my wife and coauthor of this book, Erica. We met as teenagers, married in our twenties, and raised our family by loving and working together side by side. One of Erica's core beliefs is to "Adventure on!" She keeps our family focused on seeing life as a series of wonderful adventures, each well worth experiencing to the fullest. Beyond being an amazing wife and mother, Erica is an instructor, mentor, and coach who has been an advocate for gender equity in student athletics since before we married in the summer of 1996. We have coauthored multiple bestselling books and countless articles and been guests on all types of media interviews, and together we direct an independent foundation that provides mentoring resources to schools, community groups, and family resource services around the world. Both personally and professionally, we are better together.

We count it a great privilege to share this book with you. As you read about the science, experiences, stories, and a few of our own personal opinions about parenting, please remember one thing above all else. Parents are the most significant influence in a child's life. That makes you a very important person. We know you want the best for your kids. For them to grow up to have a better life than your own. We want the same for ours. This means the privilege and responsibility we share as parents include great stewardship of the few years we are given to raise them ready.

Adventure on,
Jonathan & Erica Catherman

PART 1

READY

1. ADULTING

adult·ing
noun
The practice of behaving in a way characteristic of a responsible adult, especially the accomplishment of mundane but necessary tasks.

It's Just a Phase

Parents and pediatricians agree. Predicting the exact path and pace kids will take on their journey from childhood to adulthood is a complicated and often imprecise forecast. What begins with nine months of prenatal nurturing will not end until well after you have watched them pack up and leave your home for a life on their own.

In the whirlwind of their early years, your child's physical, mental, emotional, and social growth spins through a series of complex and often confusing developmental stages. From their first word, first step, and first day of school to their first date, first car, and first place of their own, their brains and bodies are in a near constant state of growth and change. They never are the same person more than a few days in a row.

Odd as this may sound, there were times when it felt like our own kids were growing up too slow. Especially when a dozen diaper changes a day smelled like twelve too many. Then in what felt like a blink of the eye, they started asking for cell phones, the car keys, and what it costs to rent an off-campus apartment at college. How you feel about the pace and track of your kids' development probably depends on which end of the child-rearing years you stand. Looking ahead or thinking back, we all know they can't stay young forever. Adorable babies become cute kids. Kids grow into weird and at times wonderful teens. And teens eventually graduate into the highly anticipated phase of life that in recent years has become known by the catchy title of "adulting." At least that's how the story goes in most families.

The chronicles of childhood memories told by Boomers and most Gen Xers include stories of how growing up was a buildup to accepting the many responsibilities that came with becoming an adult. Some families went as far as to mark a specific date with a traditional and often formal final step over the threshold between childhood and adulthood. Oh, how things have changed in recent years. Today, many young people see the act of adulting as a series of off-balance, social-media-documented, parent-funded, temporary test runs into adulthood. Two steps forward, one step back. No need to rush into things.

Whatever your family's expectation is for the exchange of age-related titles and behaviors, it's good to start by answering a critical question about your child: When it comes time for them to leave the nest, how prepared will they really be for life on their own?

To start this discussion, we feel it's important to make the distinction between kids who grow up into adults and kids who simply grew up. The difference between the two is night and day and evident in the desire common to parents: "All we want is for our kids to grow up into adults who are happy and healthy, and who will find purpose and success in the world." You have probably said something similar about your child. As any good parent should.

Pause for just a minute to take another look at that statement.

"All we want is for our kids to grow up into adults who are happy and healthy, and who will find purpose and success in the world."

Do you see the two similar yet separate qualities parents want for our kids? In order for them to enjoy their best life possible, they need to *grow up* and become *adults*. Technically speaking, to grow up is the progression between childhood and adulthood that includes reaching full physical and mental maturity. Having accomplished both, hopefully simultaneously, our kids should have a good shot at experiencing all the happiness, health, and a reasonable measure of success we think they deserve. Unfortunately, some kids manage to make it all the way through childhood only to find they grew up unprepared for their unavoidable adult life. That's because not all adults are grown-ups.

The distinction is not just a matter of semantics—those who are grown-ups and those who grew up. The former requires maturing in ways that shed previous childish ways of thinking and behaving. The latter simply celebrated enough birthdays to pass through puberty. They started off in a baby's body and over the following two decades grew into their physically developed adult self. All it took was time, and a lot of groceries. What the latter adults lack is maturity.

On the other hand, to become a grown-up, a child needs to develop in ways that are far more than purely physical. True grown-ups have also developed mental maturity. **Maturity comes when life lessons shape wisdom and judgment to form the mindsets, skillsets, and toolsets kids need to shed childlike dependencies for the confidence and capabilities of adult-level independence.**

We have friends our age whose kids, like our own, are all grown. With great anticipation they are setting out into the world to further their education, begin their careers, and start families of their own. They are fully grown-up—mature, independent adults. We also know families whose children grew up but failed to launch. Though their kids have reached physical and legal adulthood, they still act in ways that require others to do for them what they could or should do for themselves. They grew up into physically developed, mentally immature, dependent adults.

Can you see the difference? Attributes versus age. Independent versus dependent. Grown-up versus grew up.

It's Just a Matter of Time

Legally speaking, there is an official-sounding term used to mark the date when a young person is formally considered an adult and granted the legitimate standing of the age. Though exactly where different countries draw their lines on equal status and treatment under the law varies between nations, the same legal language is commonly recognized worldwide. When citing the collection of laws that officially grants an individual lawful control over their decisions, actions, and physical person, the most often used label for the age of formal adulthood is the *age of majority*.[1]

As one might expect, most nations in the world grant the legal age of majority to their youth in celebration of their eighteenth birthday. Yet there remain a few outliers whose religious and cultural traditions, backed by civil codes, hold open the door to legal adulthood for girls as young as nine lunar years old (eight years and nine months) and to boys who are all of fifteen lunar years.[2] The not-so-old age of fifteen solar years is good enough for a few other countries while a half dozen more officially plant the kiss of legal independence on their citizens in celebration of their sweet sixteenth birthday.[3] On the opposite end of the teen years huddles a baker's dozen count of homelands who shelter their youth until nineteen, twenty, and even twenty-one years old before allowing their minors to become full majors.

Contrary to popular belief, the United States' individual states are not all united on the official age of legal American adulthood. The majority of states, forty-seven of the fifty, agree that fresh-faced minors become legitimate adults on their eighteenth birthday.

This must feel like an unfair privilege to youths in Alabama and Nebraska, as they must wait to blow out nineteen candles before receiving full personal autonomy.[4] Tack on two more years and Mississippi takes the cake by pushing their minor's rightful bestowment of majority all the way up to twenty-one years old.[5]

To complicate matters even more, there is a second set of "age of" standards that we use to measure a person's progress on the road to adulthood. Where the age of majority provides legal *recognition* of adult status, the age of *license* provides legal permission to engage in certain acts reserved for age-specific degrees of adulting. The most obvious and often debated are when a person is granted the legal license to drive, vote, get married, and consume alcohol. The usual answers are sixteen to drive, eighteen to cast a ballot or tie the knot, and twenty-one to buy booze. That is unless . . .

. . . you are driving in one of the five states that issue licenses to teens younger, or the eleven states that require motorists to be older, than sixteen.[6]

. . . you are voting in a third of the states that allow constituents who are seventeen but will be eighteen by the general election to cast a ballot in the primaries.[7]

. . . you are getting married in one of the states where, with consent of a parent, young couples can tie the knot at the blissful ages of twelve to seventeen years old.[8]

. . . you are drinking in one of the twenty-nine states that allow minors to "partake" on private property with parental consent. Or in the six states where it's okay to down a cold one at home without mom or dad's approval. Or in the eight states that allow parents to buy their kids a round in a bar or restaurant. Or you are tipping one back in the twenty-six states where minors of all ages can partake for religious purposes, the sixteen states that allow under-age consumption for medical exemptions, the eleven states where drinking is allowed for educational purposes, or the five states where the sauce is suitable for minors who can claim they drink for work related to government purposes.[9]

Beyond the borders of the United States and depending on your global whereabouts, both the age of *majority* and the age of *license* can swing in any given direction. It really all hinges on who's currently in power legally, religiously, and culturally. In the end, there's only one state that can offer any level of consistency in measuring legal adulthood within its boundaries. The state of confusion.

As most "adults" want both their proverbial legal cake and the liberty to eat it too, the differences between age of majority and age of license have been the root of countless family quarrels and more than a few court proceedings. Here is just a sampling of opening arguments the kids we have worked with over the years have used on their parents to debate their age-frustrated demands.

"In my driver's ed class the teacher said quick reaction time and good eyesight are key to safe driving. If that's actually true, then old people shouldn't be allowed behind the wheel and young people should."

"For real. This is taxation without representation. If I'm old enough for the government to withhold taxes from my paycheck, I'm old enough to vote on how those tax dollars get spent."

"It's not fair. Nobody should be allowed to put age restrictions on love! Not my old-fashioned parents. Not the church. And definitely not some white-haired law-making politicians who don't even know me."

"So, I'm old enough to serve in the military, fight in a war, and die for my country? But not to drink a beer? How is that even logical?"

Sound familiar? If your child is currently working their way through their teen to early twentysomething years, then yes, you've probably heard a version of at least one of these claims made in your own home. That or you remember saying something very similar back when you were their age. Can't you just hear a younger version of yourself disagreeing with your parents . . .

"You have no idea! All my friends' parents let them
_____ " (insert unrealistic expectation here).

Or maybe,

"Stop treating me like a child! I'm practically an adult already!"

How about,

"How can you expect me to act more mature when I'm not allowed to do more mature things!"

And how did that work out for you? Not surprisingly we can't remember a single time as kids that any of those illogical lines changed our parent's mind. Can you recall why your wishes for early access to the privileges of adulthood weren't granted? Why didn't your parents allow you to do all those grown-up things you so desperately wanted to try? Because we were—how did they put it—"not ready yet."

Turns out that no matter how fly we were, singing along with DJ Jazzy Jeff and the Fresh Prince about how "Parents Just Don't Understand," it didn't change the fact that there is a big difference between looking the part of a grown-up and being mature enough to act like one. Even though the physical characteristics of our once young bodies may have appeared mature on the outside, on the inside our still developing brains lagged more than a few developmental steps behind. The same is true with kids today.

Out of Sync

During much of the nineteenth and twentieth centuries, many medical and education experts firmly believed that human brains wrapped up development somewhere inside our puberty years. This long-standing belief has not survived challenges from an ever-growing body of more specific and recent neural research. Studies now confirm that adolescence is the prime time for continued, not concluded, brain growth.[10] While the adolescent years quickly and obviously transform the bodies of boys and girls into young men and women, a separate sync of developmental changes is happening in their heads. Basically, grown-up bodies are built during the teen years, yet their adult minds aren't fully online until well into post-adolescence. This means that while our kids' pubescent physiques are growing up, out, and they are more interested in each other, their brain's frontal lobes' responsibility for the "executive function" of impulse control, planning, and adaptability to change may not fully mature for another ten, fifteen, or even twenty years.[11]

At this point it's very important we agree that puberty, teens, and adolescence can no longer be considered one and the same. Most members of premillennial generations were raised hearing the three youthful terms used freely and interchangeably. Like when a parent, frustrated with the behavior of their fourteen-year-old child, said to a friend something like,

> "Then again, I don't know what I was expecting. They are in the middle of _____, after all."

When we were growing up, you could have filled in the blank by inserting any one of the three words, "puberty" or "teens" or

26

"adolescence." They were all used universally to convey pretty much the same meaning.

"Then again, I don't know what I was expecting. They are in the middle of *puberty*, after all."

"Then again, I don't know what I was expecting. They are in the middle of their *teens*, after all."

"Then again, I don't know what I was expecting. They are in the middle of *adolescence*, after all."

Your pick. Puberty, teens, and adolescence. They all worked. But that was then, and this is now. Today our biological maturity (puberty), chronological age (teens), and cultural expectations (adolescence) no longer pace side by side as naturally as they once did in generations past. Like the breakup of your favorite '90s band, the three slowly separated and fell out of sync following the rise of two uniquely twenty-first-century trends in the "normal" youth experience.

First, the awkward age of puberty has somehow managed to start younger. As weird as this sounds, it's perfectly normal for our voice-cracking, acne-fighting, hormone-moody kids to experience the onset of the joys of puberty between the ages of eight and thirteen years old. That means some elementary girls as young as the fourth grade are starting their periods and many boys really should try shaving their peach fuzz mustaches prior to entering middle school.

Second, the cultural significance of being a teenager is being stretched out on both ends. Tugging down by impatient tweens whose aspirations to try what was once reserved for the older kids is drawing the age of adolescence back into the single digits. On the other end of the teen years, late-to-engage twentysomethings are stretching out adolescence as long as possible. Much to the pain of their parents, educators, and employers, many young yet legal adults are choosing to delay flying much farther than the comforts of their parents' home. Instead, they are choosing to rehearse gradually "adulting" long before making an all-in commitment to adulthood.

With such strong forces of change distorting the tween-teen-twentysomething years, social scientists are reassessing their definitions of adolescence while consumer brand marketers are hedging their bets about the future fate of what they'll call the age. Currently we can see only two possible outcomes. Either an official extension of the span of years we identify as adolescence or the eventual extinction of the stage of life all together.

Those arguing for the extension of adolescence to occupy a longer time frame often lay their reasoning, and blame, squarely at the feet of today's parents. Their primary argument states that the shift from childhood to adulthood has become overly sheltered and politicized. Softening cultural norms reinforced by the hovering protections of overindulging wannabe-woke parents has lured families into keeping the kids in happy havens, free from stress and conflict, far too long. In turn, young children are given aspirational access to adolescent behavior earlier and then allowed to shelter at home longer, well into their roaring twenties. The result is that social scientists are saying the new age of adolescence is making moving out after high school optional as twenty-five becomes the new eighteen.

Using a similar argument to reach a completely different outcome, others claim adolescence is doomed to extinction. Due to a lack of clear boundaries on previously age-appropriate experiences and an all-access pass to almost everything on the internet, many believe we will soon come to see adolescence as an obsolete age of the pre-web world. What had been previously reserved for real-life experiences has become a mostly unsupervised online search-and-click through a virtual world for the young and curious.

What becomes of the age of adolescence is still up in the air and will not be officially determined for some time to come. Important to us today is that we see the clear distinctions between puberty, the teen years, and adolescence. This will help us to better prepare our children to thrive in the challenges of each, while increasing our understanding of why and how they'll respond to the demands of life on their own. How prepared they are with the mindset, skillset, and toolset needed to succeed away from the protection your parenting wings provide will determine if they are ready, or not, to soar on their own.

Terms to take into consideration:

Kid is a child or young person of any age.

Child is a son or daughter of any age. The term also refers to a young person below the age of puberty or below the legal age of majority. Child can also be used to describe an immature or irresponsible person.

Puberty is when a child's body begins to physically and sexually mature in a process that transforms them into an adult.

Tween is a young person between the ages of approximately eight and twelve years old.

Teenager is a young person between thirteen and nineteen years old.

Adolescence is the transition period between childhood and adulthood and is derived from a Latin word meaning "to grow up or to grow into maturity." In 1904, Stanley Hall, president of the American Psychological Association, described a new developmental phase that arose after a series of significant social changes occurred at the turn of the twentieth century.[12] New child labor laws and universal education meant kids had more available free time and

29

fewer of the responsibilities that had previously been expected and even forced on them as teenagers.

Adult is a person after the age of majority as specified by law.

Adulting is the practice of behaving in a way characteristic of a responsible adult, especially the accomplishment of mundane but necessary tasks.

Adulthood is the period in a person's lifespan after adolescence.

Grow up is the progression between childhood and adulthood that includes developing physical and mental maturity.

Grown-up is a physically and mentally mature adult.

Grew up is to have completed physical development.

2. READY OR NOT

More Than a Game

"One, two, three, four . . . ninety-eight, ninety-nine, one hundred! Ready or not, here I come!"

The odds are pretty good that your mind just wandered back in time to the warm evenings of childhood. Remember when playing outside with friends was the best part of the day? Free from the concerns of school, chores, or making a mess of the house, we ran through side yards, backyards, cul-de-sacs, and wooded lots, pushing the limits of dusk to finish just one more round of the greatest game ever played: hide-and-seek.

As all kids with skinned knees and dirty hands will agree, the best or worst moments in every game happen at the same time, early in play. Either a sense of great pride or heart-sinking fear grabs hold of players when they hear the "it" kid conclude their count, uncover their eyes, and holler at the top of their voice, "Ready or not, here I come!"

For those who have found the perfect hiding spot, yes, they are ready. Then there are the other kids. Exposed, they find themselves still searching under, over, or between just about anything for cover. To those kids, in that moment, nothing could feel worse. Because no, they are not ready.

These memories are a good analogy for what we parents know the future holds for our children. The countdown at home base is just a few numbers from concluding and the demands of the world will soon be seeking them out. It's best to be confident that they are in a good spot when the booming voice of life demands, "Ready or not, here I come."

Unlike the carefree games we enjoyed playing as kids, the adult life of parenting proves to be a bit more intense. One day it feels like you are winning and the very next morning you want to tap out before breakfast and maybe, or maybe not, try again tomorrow. As legendary boxer Joe Louis told his opponent Billy Conn on the eve of their heavyweight championship fight, "You can run, but you can't hide."[1] Our children may think they can run from or avoid the responsibilities of growing up for a time, but the bags under our eyes prove there really is no place they can hide from the heavy-hitting demands of life. That is, unless your parenting plan includes sheltering adult children in place and providing on-demand meal, laundry, and evening turndown services. Not an option? Good. So now what?

Pick a Path

Over the years we have been privileged to work with some very high-capacity people and their families. A few of our most memorable events have included speaking before audiences of professional athletes, elite military operators, first responders, and K20 educators. Each engagement not only provides a unique opportunity for us to share insights about bridging the gap between generations but also grants us an extremely valuable occasion to learn more about what prepares some people to thrive in situations that others merely hope to survive.

Undoubtedly, it takes an extraordinary kind of person to win world championships, conduct covert operations, answer emergency calls for help, and effectively inspire all types of learning.

In our investigation into what makes these elite performers tick, we often refer to models that assess people's responses to tough situations and how they view the experience, as well as provide insight into their potential performance outcomes. Remarkably, one such measure not only applies to assessing the likelihood of success in feats of great demand but, with a little tweaking, can be used to assist parents in determining how well prepared their kids are to set out on their own in the not-too-distant future.

For the sake of simplicity, we call this model the Readiness Assessment. Its purpose is to guide us in gaining insight into which path our kids are likely to follow when facing the many unavoidable demands of life. This can include simple tasks like doing chores, cooking meals, and waking up on time to get to school before the first bell. On their own. The model can also be applied to the more trying requirements of adulthood, like finding and renting an apartment, managing money, maintaining a car, and gaining a firm grasp on the holy grail of independence—getting and keeping a job.

Warning: The next few paragraphs are going to feel a little bit textbookish. But stick with us for a minute and we promise to translate the complex scientific language of interdisciplinary models examining the interconnections between biology, psychology, and socioenvironmental factors into something easily understood by parents without a PhD in developmental psychology. The brief effort will be well worth the read.

To set up the Readiness Assessment model for success in parenting, we need to look back on its inspiration. In physiology and psychology there exists a well-validated theoretical model known as the biopsychosocial (BPS) model of challenge and threat, describing the relationship between psychological processes and physiological responses.[2] There are multiple variations of the theory, all based on the same basic structure, which looks something like this:

First applied in the research of measuring cardiovascular responses during active goal pursuits, this BPS model has taken on another life far beyond the lab. Coaches have repurposed it with athletes in locker room pep talks, and teachers with students studying to pass final exams. Even college students in dorm laundry rooms are unknowingly assessing how they'll respond to messy situations based on how prepared—or unprepared—they are to separate, wash, dry, and fold.

Now, if that sterile-looking forked-path BPS framework leaves you uninspired to dive into the deep waters of social psychology, don't worry, the feeling is a common one. It just means you are a perfectly normal parent. Instead, we'll make things as relevant as possible by presenting you with our designed-for-parents reinterpretation of the model. Below you'll find the Readiness Assessment, followed by a brief explanation.

Obviously, our Readiness Assessment looks much different than the traditional BPS model we bored you with a page back. Whereas the standard BPS model is used to evaluate performance outcomes based on the body's cardiovascular responses to demand and resource evaluations, the Readiness Assessment uses qualities of your kid's maturity to help predict their future performance. The two essential values we pay attention to in the Readiness Assessment are your kid's willingness and ability to effectively engage in the many real-life demands—both expected and unpredictable—that all adults face.

In simpler than scientific terms, think about the Readiness Assessment like this. When we find ourselves facing a task that re-

In Real Life

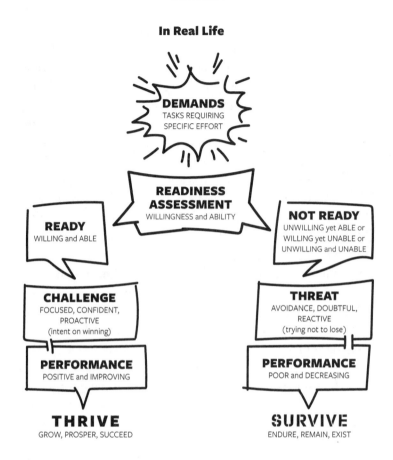

quires a specific effort (DEMAND), the first thing we do is size up the situation (READINESS ASSESSMENT). Based on our resources (WILLINGNESS and ABILITY), we determine how stressed we feel (CHALLENGE or THREAT) and predict an outcome (PERFORMANCE) that will then define the overall experience (THRIVE or SURVIVE).

At first glance, the Readiness Assessment seems like a worded stripped-down version of the world-famous game called Plinko. Made popular by the iconic daytime television game show *The Price Is Right*, the Plinko game is played by releasing Plinko chips (like a hockey puck) down the vertical game board. As the chips fall, they randomly bounce off rows of evenly distributed pegs, making a *plink, plink, plink* sound all the way down. At the bottom of the wall, Plinko chips land in a prize slot. Brought to life by the show's executive producer Frank Wayne, Plinko quickly became the most popular segment. Though Mr. Wayne is credited with the game's invention, such an imaginative concept for contestants to "come on down"—to win cash prizes and lose their minds—didn't come to him at random. The essence of Plinko's entertainment factor is known in the study of probability and statistics as *binomial distribution*, demonstrated by another pegged board device called a Galton board. The Plinko game gets cheers from viewers and a Galton board gets analyzed by scientists—both for their random probability of success or failure through experimentation.

Getting back to the Readiness Assessment, rest assured, it is neither an experiment to run on your kids nor a game of chance to play with their future. The direction your child takes at the intersections in the Readiness Assessment can be both a somewhat predictable decision and an accurate measure of how prepared your child currently is to deal with the many demands of life.

3. THE READINESS ASSESSMENT

IRL

Let's take it from the top. Our introduction to the Readiness Assessment begins in a place where most people spend a lot of their time—In Real Life.

This slang phrase sprang to existence in the early days of the internet. The term was originally used by people who needed to distinguish the differences between what was happening in the virtual world from experiences IRL, In Real Life.

As real life would have it, it didn't take long for the abbreviated term to catch on off-line as well. Migrating far beyond its inter-web origin, IRL became a welcome-back-to-reality description of what truly exists beyond our mental, physical, and emotional escapisms.

Some of our favorite escapes from reality have become IRL adulting memes. These funny pics include quippy text that often cuts to the irony of what we are all thinking. There's the picture of a beautifully plated dish of food under the caption "Dinner Plans." Beside it mirrors a dimly lit image of a pot of water set on a stovetop over the caption "Turned on the wrong burner and have been cooking nothing for 20 minutes." That's IRL. Then there are the countless memes of a cat under a blanket, a child sleeping awkwardly on the stairs, or a straw stabbed into a box of wine, framed by the statement, *I'm done adulting for the day.*

Judging by the popularity of such posts on social media, there are a lot of thirty-, forty-, fifty-something adults who wish to escape from the ever present and at times all too exhausting demands of adulthood. IRL.

Unfortunately, there are only a few true escapes from the déjà vu demands of life beyond childhood. There always seems to be one more load of laundry or stack of dishes to clean, or hide . . . IRL.

Yep, they've scheduled another mandatory work meeting, redundant report, and training to complete . . . IRL.

There's no pressing pause on a sick child, lost pet, and car making a strange *clunk whir hiss* sound—again, all at the same time . . . IRL.

In Real Life is the source of an ever-flowing river of can't-be-ignored demands.

Grocery shopping, sports practice, homework help, doctor appointments, vet bills, congested commutes, home maintenance, music recitals, lunch appointments, and "please God no not another" IRL school fee. Meme that!

Let's face the facts. There is no end to the seemingly infinite flow of In Real Life demands. They are simply an undeniable part of every day. This is not to say the demands of life are all bad. Many are vital as an invaluable source of growth and potential benefit. This makes our In Real Life demands the headwater source of our Readiness Assessment.

Demands

de·mands
noun
The urgent requests or requirements in life that necessitate specific effort.

The demands of life are surprisingly numerous and remarkably persistent. They usually insist on being the center of attention and, more often than not, get their way. An adult's lifetime of experience will confirm that no matter how much time and effort is dedicated to planning, the unexpected demands tend to have the worst timing. And when an unforeseen demand forces its way into the day, it rarely goes away until it has been dealt with properly or has exacted a hefty toll.

The demands we face daily come at us in every imaginable shape, size, and degree. For instance, grocery shopping is one of the many predictable required tasks of life. Whereas discovering that your vehicle's back left tire is flat *after* you have already loaded the groceries into the trunk—well, that was a surprise. Both grocery shopping and a flat tire are considered demands that necessitate a specific effort to address and resolve.

Here are a few more examples of everyday demands that shouldn't be ignored:

- Getting enough sleep
- Leaving for work or school on time
- Completing a W-4 form when starting a new job
- Checking and responding to email
- Fixing a flushed yet not draining toilet bowl
- Replacing a burned-out car headlight
- Making and keeping a doctor appointment
- Reviewing bank statements
- Paying bills on or before their due date
- Cleaning living spaces

Basically, any situation that requires a specific effort to address can be considered a demand. For a responsible person, this makes perfect sense. When life happens, a prepared person can face almost any demand. They do what it takes to manage the situation and move on. Whereas the unprepared person may find the same situation too hard to handle. They might choose to avoid, ignore, or outright deny that the demand even exists. Knowingly or not, both people are now fully engaged in a personal Readiness Assessment and will soon head down opposite paths toward two very different outcomes.

Readiness Assessment

The Readiness Assessment is a very straightforward evaluation. It poses two simple questions to determine who is adequately prepared and ready and who is unprepared and not ready to face a specific demand.

Question 1: Are you *willing* to take on the demand?
Question 2: Are you *able* to take on the demand?

Willingness is a measure of one's mindset. Ability is the combination of a person's skillset and toolset. Think of your own child. Consider for a minute how ready they are to take on specific day-to-day demands of life. Like completing their chores or turning in their schoolwork. What about their personal care or the requirements of a part-time job? How willing are they to engage with the demands and are they able to do what is required? Of course, the answer can vary greatly between children and demands. Their willingness and ability can depend on their age, maturity, exposures, experiences, practices, and the expectations placed on them up to this point in life.

We will dive into the details of how willingness and ability are developed in part 2 of this book. Before we go there, it's important to consider what willingness and ability are made of and how each determines whether your kid is ready or not for life on their own.

Are You Ready for This?

"I was born ready!"

Once the confident comeback of movie heroes, "I was born ready" has become an overused retort of mixed humor, sarcasm, and eye-roll-worthy overstatement of self-assurance. There's just one very big problem with the saying. No matter how confidently it's delivered, nothing could be further from the truth. No one, not a single person, ever, has been born ready. It's simply physically impossible.

The reason nobody has ever been born ready is easily understood yet often forgotten after the last high-school-level natural science exam you thought you'd ever see. So, here's a quick reminder of what you probably circled in your class notes because the teacher said it would absolutely be on the test.

Homo sapiens are what biologists call an altricial species. Humans are considered highly intelligent Homo sapiens, yet like all altricial species, our young are underdeveloped at the time of birth and require considerable attention for many years. Basically, our babies are born pretty much helpless. They are totally Not Ready for anything close to managing on their own. Which all exhausted parents know far too well.

Okay, the biology refresher lesson is over. If we were reminded of one thing in today's lecture, it's that no human child was ever "born ready." So the next time you hear someone say, "I was born ready," you can translate their greatly overstated proclamation of self-confidence into what they actually mean: "I am willing."

41

With a capital W. Admittedly, "I am Willing" doesn't have quite the same ring to it as "I was born ready" does. Still, willing is an actual thing and a critical component of your child's Readiness, so we'll take it.

Willingness = Mindset

Willingness is all about Mindset. When facing one of life's many demands, a kid with a "can-do" mindset is open to trying new things and repeating what they hope to improve upon. From a five-year-old eager to tie their own shoes to a teenager wanting to set their own dentist appointment, **a willing mindset isn't about already knowing how to do something; it's about making an attempt and practicing ways to get better.**

Of course, the opposite of willing also exists. When we hear a child whine or a teen huff in your general direction, "But I don't wanna," they are giving voice to their *un*willing mindset. Sure, an eight-year-old really should be capable of making themselves a sandwich for lunch. Any teenager who has started a YouTube channel should also be clever enough to run a load of laundry. But ask any tenured parent, and you'll hear that when a child has made up their mind they don't want to do something, finding a way through their strong will can require some skillful parenting and maybe a bit of thoughtful "negotiating."

Mindset is such a strong factor in a Readiness Assessment that it directly influences the quality and quantity of one's abilities. Parents who describe their kids as *determined, stubborn, fixated,* or *obsessed* have probably also said of their child that "where there's a will, there's a way," "when their mind is made up, there's no stopping them," and "if they want something bad enough, nothing will get in their way." A child with a resolved mindset can be absolutely unstoppable at times. On the sheer brute force of their willingness, they are bound to get through a lot in life. But if they really want to go far, they'll also need to channel some of their willing determination into building a solid set of effective and efficient abilities.

Ability = Skillset + Toolset

Ability is the combination of two separate yet equally important assets, Skillsets and Toolsets. Not to cast shade on motivational posters and inspirational social media posts, but most fail to mention how important ability is to your child's success in school, sports, work, and almost everything in life. It turns out that despite all the hype, attitude *isn't* everything. Yes, a willing attitude is important. But so is your child's ability to effectively address the demands of life with a certain degree of specific task performance.

In addition to a willing Mindset—#attitude—kids need to be prepared with a solid combination of a practiced Skillset and ever important Toolset needed to address specific demands. We will dive deeper into how mindset, skillset, and toolset are built in part 2 of the book. Until then, please highlight, underline, or circle the next two sentences. There is only one combination of Willingness (Mindset) plus Ability (Skillset and Toolset) that will prepare your kids to succeed in building a life of their own, away from your home. On the other hand, there are multiple insufficient mixtures of Mindset, Skillset, and Toolset that will leave them unprepared and Not Ready to leave your nest.

More than being in the right place at the right time, Ready allows any place to be the right place and anytime to be the right time to shine. Here is a fun example of what Ready looks like when a kid is both willing and able to face a demand, when the time comes.

Child's Play

You know the players are having fun when the tennis match commentators are obviously enjoying themselves too.

"We've got a challenge here for Roger. Grigor will pass the baton to a young guy here. Looks like he's ready to go."[1]

Ready to go. What a statement. Especially when we realize that professional tennis player Grigor Dimitrov has just stepped off the court and been replaced by a "ready to go" twelve-year-old kid. Wearing jeans and a hoodie, the unknown tween is encouraged by the cheers of the match spectators as he confidently walks onto the court, stands racket in hand, and readies himself to receive a rocket served over the net from the legend himself, Roger the GOAT Federer.

Yah, yah. Roger Federer. Sure, he's arguably the greatest tennis player of all time. But who's the underdressed kid and why is he subbing for Grigor, right in the middle of a match?

A hush falls over the crowd.

Federer coils and serves.

Kid returns the Swiss master's offering with a confident forehand.

Federer drops back and spins the ball's return just inches over the net.

Kid runs, slides, and stretches with a smart retort and keeps the rally alive.

Federer rushes the net, forcing the kid to sprint for the far side of the court.

Kid answers by striking a powerful backhand return.

Federer pounds back his reply.

Kid finishes off the seventeen-time Grand Slam champion with a perfectly executed overhand lob that lands just inside the baseline.

Point!

And the crowd goes wild!

How exactly does an unheralded preteen kid come out of the stands and successfully volley against one of the world's most accomplished tennis legends? At this point it doesn't matter that the Madison Square Garden venue was an exhibition match. Hearing the cheers rising from the spectators, you would have thought they were courtside for a world-championship dual. What matters is, when the boy was offered the opportunity to play across the net from the best of the best, he was both willing and able to play the champ. Turns out, he was exactly as the commentators described: "Ready to go."

The critical combination of willingness (Mindset) and ability (Skillset + Toolset) prepared the young tennis player to accept the challenge of competing on the same court as the big boys. Then again, what if the kid didn't know how to play tennis? Or he had the practiced skill yet lacked a tennis racket? Or what if he knew how to play, had a racket in hand, but wasn't willing to face the great Roger Federer? The outcome would have been much different. But instead, he was both willing to be there and able to take on the greatest demand of his young tennis-playing life. The same goes for every type of demand the kid—and your kid—will face in life. An ample mindset, skillset, and toolset prepares them for success when opportunity (demand) serves.

Challenge or Threat

CHALLENGE	THREAT
FOCUSED, CONFIDENT, PROACTIVE	AVOIDANCE, DOUBTFUL, REACTIVE
(intent on winning)	(trying not to lose)

An interesting thing happens in our child's head once a Ready or Not Ready verdict has been determined. Those who are Ready (willing and able) experience the feeling of challenge, while those who are Not Ready can feel threatened. Interestingly, you know what our brains love? A good challenge. You know what our brains hate? Almost any threat.

The brains of kids who are Ready tend to focus on the benefits of taking on a demand. Not Ready kids often feel out of control and fear making mistakes.

Ready kids play to win. Not Ready kids are often just trying not to lose.

Ready is proactive and confident. Not Ready is reactive and doubtful.

Ready kids perceive more of their emotions to be positive and beneficial to their performance. Not Ready kids tend to have more negative emotions and believe their feelings will adversely affect their ability to perform adequately.

Performance

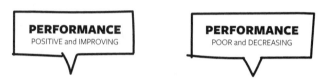

Kids experience very different performance behaviors and potential outcomes depending on if they are Ready for the Challenge or Not Ready for the Threat.

In a Challenge state, our emotional and physical responses tend to be positive, which contributes to good performance. The advantages of the positive physical and emotional responses of the Challenge state include improved decision-making, elevated task engagement, disciplined self-regulation, elevated anaerobic power, and more interest in increasing one's mindset, skillset, and toolset.

The positive responses to the Challenge state help explain *why* your kid looks and feels so relaxed when they are in their groove, they've got their game on, or you can just see that this is totally their thing. Time just seems to fly by. It's like they could do this all day, every day. If you'd only let them.

Then there is what happens to us when we are Not Ready and find ourselves feeling threatened. When experiencing a Threat state, our emotional and physiological responses are typically negative and often lead to unfavorable outcomes. The disadvantages of a negative physical and emotional response to a Threat state are many. Cognitive function decreases. We experience a decrease in task engagement. More resources are devoted to self-regulation. We focus on prevention and distress while showing disinterest in advancement of Mindset, Skillset, and Toolset.

The negative responses to the Threat state help reveal why our kids hate doing things they don't like.

They can't seem to get anything right.

You are making them do it.

They feel like this is taking forever.

They would rather take the F grade, sit out the next game, or be grounded forever than be forced to waste one more second on this.

It's so *stupid*.

We also know this type of behavior as *fight or flight*.

Here's a Challenge vs. Threat performance summary in only two sentences: **Those who are Ready to face the Demands of life feel Challenged and tend to perform required tasks well. Those who are Not Ready to face the Demands of life feel Threatened and often perform required tasks poorly.**

Thriving versus Surviving

THRIVE	**SURVIVE**
GROW, PROSPER, SUCCEED	ENDURE, REMAIN, EXIST

In the early first century AD, the Roman Stoic philosopher Seneca wrote to his young learners, "Let all your efforts be directed to something, let it keep that end in view."[2] Though his work dates back to somewhere between AD 49 and 62, the idea of beginning with the end in mind is usually a good way to start and remains true today. Think about the value of this assertion from your kid's point of view. If you were to ask them if they want to do well at home, in school, with friends, and in their personal interests, how would they answer? Without question they would choose to thrive.

Who wouldn't want to grow, prosper, and succeed? The alternative certainly isn't very appealing.

To thrive or to survive, that is the question. Although the determination of thrive or survive appears at the end of the Readiness Assessment, the decision is often made much earlier. In many ways it is forecast from the beginning. The kids who are Ready to face life's many Demands are on track to Thrive. Those who are Not Ready? Well, don't worry, surely they'll Survive.

Survive? It just sounds so pessimistic when said like that. Doesn't it? Maybe we are overstating it. Or perhaps we are just sneaking a peek at the elephant in the room. Few parents want to admit that their kids are underprepared and may be at a disadvantage when it comes to experiencing the future benefits Ready makes accessible. Especially if they end up lacking some of the abilities (Skillset + Toolset) required to thrive. Ones that could have been developed well in advance of facing life's many Demands.

Same Storm, Different Boats

It became clear early in the COVID-19 pandemic that though people around the world were all weathering the same storm (Demands), we were not all in the same boat. Global closures of schools, workplaces, travel, and most social events forced us all to quickly start living very different lives. But what "different" ended up meaning to children in homes, schools, and communities with ample resources to manage the new normal proved to be smooth sailing compared to what many disadvantaged children experienced. Though few people were truly prepared in the beginning, those who had the means to quickly ready themselves for the demands of a pandemic managed the disruptions in ways that might be compared to how a sound ship weathers high seas. Despite the unpredictable waves, many were still able to safely ride out the storm, make forward progress, and in some cases even *thrive* in their challenging circumstances.

Then there were the kids with no safe harbor. Adrift in the equivalent of a rickety raft, millions of disadvantaged children fought to simply *survive* as they fell behind academically, socially, and emotionally. In just a matter of weeks, even days, millions of kids lost what little securities they could rely on and drifted powerless, barely afloat, through increasingly threatening conditions at home, in online schooling, and in their shuttered communities.

Do you see the difference between *thrive* and *survive*? Perhaps it's too easy to make the distinction between the two when we look through the powerful lens of a global pandemic. What about under more "normal" circumstances? After all, what are the chances that we will face another drastic situation where so many find themselves in so far over their head? We hope the odds are ever in our favor.

Let's be a little more everyday here. After all, with roadside assistance only a dash-button push away and everything there is to know about how to do anything held in the digital palm of their hands, how rough will our kid's future really be? It isn't like not knowing how to politely hold a soup spoon or failing to give the boss two weeks' notice before quitting a job is the end of the world. And you know what? It isn't. But those who can and do will hold a myriad of small advantages over those who don't. A few little gains here, a few more there, and before you know it, the road to Thrive is well paved in countless small pros. In the end, those who thrive can look back and see that Ready was absolutely the best place to begin.

The *Readiness* Assessment

In Real Life

DEMANDS
TASKS REQUIRING
SPECIFIC EFFORT

**READINESS
ASSESSMENT**
WILLINGNESS and ABILITY

READY
WILLING and ABLE

NOT READY
UNWILLING yet ABLE or
WILLING yet UNABLE or
UNWILLING and UNABLE

CHALLENGE
FOCUSED, CONFIDENT,
PROACTIVE
(intent on winning)

THREAT
AVOIDANCE, DOUBTFUL,
REACTIVE
(trying not to lose)

PERFORMANCE
POSITIVE and IMPROVING

PERFORMANCE
POOR and DECREASING

THRIVE
GROW, PROSPER, SUCCEED

SURVIVE
ENDURE, REMAIN, EXIST

PART 2

SET

4. MINDSET

mind·set

noun

a mental attitude, disposition, or inclination

You Just Have to Believe

How many times have you bent down, looked into your child's unsure eyes, held their hands, and told them, "You just have to believe in yourself. I believe in you. I know you can do it." Probably more times than you can remember.

Now, focus on a specific occasion when "You just have to believe" actually worked. Why did it work? Have you ever thought about how exactly you successfully managed to convince your kid that they really could do what just moments before they weren't so certain about? Maybe all they needed was a little extra encouragement. A nudge in the right direction. Or perhaps their tipping point from *can't do* to *can do* had less to do with you and more to do with their being reminded of the abilities they already possess. Whatever the reason, your child was blessed to have you right there when they decided, yes, they are ready to jump on in, all on their own.

The significance between believing and not believing in our abilities can be the difference between sinking or swimming—literally.

SET

Like when our close friend's granddaughter was convinced she couldn't jump from the side of the pool into water that was way over her head. Considering her young age, this was a good thing, which kept her away from the water's edge unless supervised by an adult. But on this day, her mom, grandmother, and Erica were all there, and it was time for her to take the plunge on her own. She had been in swim lessons for months, knew the basic strokes, was wearing floaties, and was within an arm's reach of three adults already in the cool water. Yet, with her childlike fear outweighing her abilities as a swimmer, she was certain her head would go under and she'd sink.

Shivering from doubt, she stood at the side of the pool, hesitant to make the jump. Despite all the encouragement, her little feet were glued to the pool deck.

Encouragement rained down on her from all who watched.

"We know you can do it! Just jump."

That's when she asked, "Why? How do you know I can do it?" What a great question for a child to ask those she trusts.

"Have you ever jumped into your mom's arms in the pool?" She smiled and bobbed her head up and down.

"Do you know how to swim?"

"Yes," she replied in her sweet, shy voice.

"Can you blow bubbles with your face under the water?"

"Yes, I can."

"Then we know you can do it because you know how to jump, swim, and blow bubbles when your face goes under."

"I can do it. I can do it. I can do it," she whispered to herself over and over again. Then all at once she clenched her little fists, bent her knees, and made the leap. Under she went, and up again she swam. Sputtering and giggling, she doggie-paddled toward her mother while proclaiming, "I did it. I did it. I knew I could do it!"

All she needed was a reminder of the many things she already knew how to do in the water. Putting them together gave her mind the confidence needed to believe she was up for the challenge and would not sink. Perhaps you have a similar memory of teaching a child to jump in over their head. Though the water is deep, they are perfectly capable of keeping afloat and enjoying themselves at the same time.

Now think about the countless situations that are yet to come when your child will need to believe in their abilities in order to jump into the deep end, rise up, and succeed. Only you'll be nowhere near if they reach out for assistance. How will they rally? Lift themselves up? Pull on their big-kid pants to take control of their abilities and handle the situation? If you aren't there to motivate them, how will they find what they need to believe in their own capacity to achieve? We teach kids to swim for many reasons, one of which is so that when they are around water, they don't have to rely on an adult to keep their head above the surface. Of course, swimming can also be tons of fun. So diving into the deep end requires our kids to be both confident and capable, which converts a potentially hazardous situation into an opportunity to truly enjoy themselves. What a great combo.

Unlocking Potential

In the simplest of ways, what we are talking about here is self-efficacy—your kid's no-parent-needed belief in their own capabilities to control their personal performances and in turn the events that affect their life. Sound familiar? In the Readiness Assessment, those who are both willing and able qualify as Ready. Kids who are Ready to face the demands of life trust in their abilities and are willing to use them when required. This makes Ready kids self-efficacy kids.

So not to cause any confusion, **it's important to remember that self-efficacy and self-esteem are not the same thing.** Yes, it's important that your child builds a strong sense of self-esteem, but they'll need much more than good feelings to become truly Ready. Self-efficacy is your child's founded belief that they have the skills needed to navigate forward and accomplish their goals. Such strong beliefs are linked to numerous benefits that directly apply to your child's daily life, like building healthy lifestyle habits, increased academic success, and improved workplace performance. Perhaps most important, self-efficacy fuels resilience to adversity and stress.[1] Now we're talking.

Knowing that adversity and stress are inevitable facts of life, what parent wouldn't want their child to build resilience? More than bouncing back from difficult situations, resilient kids tap into their physical, emotional, and mental growth and maturity to bounce *forward*. Well, sad to say, some parents believe their child was born without an ounce of resilience in their body and the chances are nil that they will gain any in this life. They have made up their mind their kid will not change and, short of a miracle, they are who they are, bless their heart.

This way of thinking could be called *fixed mindset parenting*. A fixed mindset holds to the belief that personal attributes and abilities, or the lack thereof, will not grow or change. They are set. From birth. If they're not good at sports, they'll never be good at sports. If they struggle with reading, they'll forever stumble through every book. If they fear speaking before a group, they're doomed to a sweaty . . . umm . . . yah . . . so umm . . . public humiliation. Every time. Basically, a fixed mindset believes that what you see is what you get.

On the other hand are parents who believe in fostering a growth mindset in themselves and their kids. A growth mindset believes that over time a person can increase what they know and what they can do. A person with a growth mindset is open to additional learning, rehearsal, and feedback, all in an attempt to improve. Simply, a growth mindset believes that we are all an evolving, ever-changing, work in progress—for the better.

Thankfully, our mindsets are not totally set in stone. As we have all experienced, people regularly change their minds. And we're not just talking about what they want to eat for dinner or if they like a certain outfit or not. We can think differently about our understandings and abilities depending on the circumstances and outside influences. This is why parents with a flexible perspective about how people discover and develop themselves are such a powerful force on their kids establishing a strong growth mindset.

How you begin laying the building blocks of self-efficacy and a growth mindset in your child's life depends a great deal on when and to what degree their young malleable minds are introduced to the benefits.

When a child cries and a parent responds with care, they naturally feel a sense of self-efficacy. A toddler who is encouraged to explore, play, discover, and practice basic skills is exposed to environments that develop self-efficacy. Children and adolescents who are purposefully given responsibility, choices, and regular opportunities to repeat experiences that hone their skills are building self-efficacy.

Likewise, your kid's growth mindset is encouraged to develop when they know a parent believes in them and their future potential. When a child hears more affirmation given to their specific efforts, hard work, and commitment to self-improvement than praise for the final reward, their growth mindset deepens. As families talk openly about their unique opportunities to develop, set goals, hold each other accountable for growth, and celebrate their accomplishments together, growth mindsets are strengthened.

The opportunities for your kid to build upon the foundation of self-efficacy and a growth mindset are vast and multifaceted. Starting young, your kid will benefit greatly from mastery experiences, vicarious experiences, verbal persuasion, and emotional and physical states of health.[2] In simpler terms, **your son or daughter will need to do, see, hear, and feel for themselves what it's like to experience both success and failure.** Again, it's best to start making deposits into these accounts as early as possible, because what kids believe about who they are, what they can do, and who they will become in the future is rooted in their mindset.

The beauty of your kid's flexible mindset stems from within the most remarkable suite of cells in the human body—their brain. To help us better understand where their furiously developing mind is coming from, let's briefly look into what's going on between their ears and how their amazing brain influences their perception of the world, both inside and out.

Under Construction

On the day your child was born, they were placed in your loving arms as an incomplete person. The reality is, they were delivered only partially constructed. This is not to say infants need printed instructions reminding parents that their little bundle of joy comes with "Some assembly required." Rather, their tiny bodies and large brains have a lot of fabricating, networking, and connecting yet to be completed.

Of the two-part manufacturing process we know as growth, your child's body and brain development are not always tracking along at the same pace. As we discussed in chapter 1, there can be a significant difference between the rate of your child's physical development and their mental maturity.

Think of their brain as mission control for their body. As the brain's systems come online, their data processing power will regularly be updated and refreshed to meet the changing needs and performance potential of your child's physical form. In other words, as they grow, there will be times when kids act older than they look and times when they look older than they act.

When our son Cole was five years old, he was a very tall kid. On his first day of kindergarten, he stood a full head taller than any of his classmates. Throughout his first year in the school building, he was often mistaken for a much older student. By the end of the school year, Cole had grown to stand head and shoulders over his friends. Literally. Though he outpaced them in physical growth, he learned from the same kindergarten curriculum at the same pace and passed the same learning milestones as his classmates. He played the same chase games on the playground and giggled at the same silly jokes while sitting criss-cross applesauce on the carpet squares. Which meant he thought and acted like the other kids in his kindergarten class.

All this was well and good at school. But when our family went to the park or out to dinner, away from his teachers and friends in class, people didn't think this tall, skinny kid acted like he looked at all. That's because he looked ten-year-old kids in the eye and he wore shoes big enough to double as water skis. But he was still a kindergartner in thought and action, though not in appearance. We even considered having a shirt custom printed for him that read "Give me a break, I'm only 5."

Eventually kids' mismatched bodies and brains find each other in the same place, at the same time. But the journey to that blessed meeting point has to pass through many stages, and the day of their union doesn't happen until late in the developmental game. To better understand how the mindset of a child is developed, let's take a quick look into what is going on inside the heads of both your youngster and teenage children. This will give us some important insight into what they are thinking and how different parenting styles can have a significant influence on the willingness of their developing mindset.

A Mind of Their Own

At birth, an infant's brain is one-quarter the size of its future adult self. In the first year of life, a child's brain will bulk up and more than double in size to about 60 percent of its full-grown potential. Between your child's first birthday and their first day of school, their brain will flourish with growth, but it will not finish developing into a fully formed thinking machine until after celebrating a still distant mid-twentysomething birthday.

Between birth and early adolescence, the two fist-sized, walnut-looking hemispheres of a young brain undergo an extensive network routing and rerouting project. This includes what brain researchers call "experience expectant" and "experience dependent" wiring.[3] Atop an extensive network of "experience independent" wiring, which functions as preset circuits controlling the body's basic abilities like breathing, heartbeat, and digestion, the experience expectant and experience dependent neural connections are determined by the influences specific to your child's environmental surroundings. Basically, the brain's life-support systems (experience independent) come prewired, while the quality-of-life networks (experience expectant and experience dependent) are yet to be established. Experience expectant wiring is the brain creating neural connections networked through "normal" environmental influences, while experience dependent ones are established entirely on the quality of the environmental input. Put in oversimplified terms, a young brain is made to learn, and what it learns depends a great deal on what it is exposed to.

The Middle Years

During adolescence, the period of time between the onset of puberty and the early to mid twenties, the brain undergoes an extensive and sometimes violent remodeling project. In addition to a fresh and frenzied growth of neural extensions, unused and inefficient neural pathways are rerouted or *pruned* away. Like a master topiary gardener trims off undesirable branches, *synaptic pruning* is the adolescent brain undergoing billions of snips and clips of the electrical and chemical signal pathways between the highly specialized neuron cells. Since neurons are the building blocks of the brain and control our thoughts, decisions, imagination, and perception of the world around us, this pruning process is incredibly important and well worth protecting. This requires the pathways that remain unpruned to be carefully shielded in a protective biochemical wrap called *myelin* through a highly orchestrated process called *myelination*.

To explain the importance of myelination sheathing in the young brain, you will need to think a little less like a parent and a lot more like an electrician. Unless you are an electrical contractor who is the parent of a teenager, this part should really spark your interest.

Most everyone has a healthy respect for electricity. You don't need to have a diagnosed case of electrophobia (the fear of electricity) to be wary of the jolt that comes with touching a bare live wire. As comedic electrician puns go, a slight zap just means you are grounded. Tradesman joking aside, to avoid such a shocking experience, sheathing surrounds electrical wires to insulate the line and keep the current moving through the cord rather than your hand. Likewise, the protective sheathing myelination adds to the non-pruned neurons in an adolescent's head is like the plastic-coated wire on your reading lamp. Both perform similar insulating functions.

Brain neurons with a myelin sheath surrounding their axons are called *white matter*. This is due to the high lipid fat content of the myelin protein that appears whitish in color while the unwrapped cells look more gray when viewed under a microscope.

Properly protected white matter neurons are highly efficient at delivering signals through the brain. How efficient? About one hundred times more efficient than non-insulated gray matter pathways. Non-insulated neurons transmit their signals at about 1 meter per second whereas insulated neurons convey their message at around 100 meters per second. To put insulated vs. non-insulated neuron signal delivery rates into perspective, consider these speed comparisons. A peregrine falcon dives at about 100 meters per second,[4] while 1 meter per second is the top pace of a speed-walking penguin.[5] A Porsche 911 tops out at about 100 meters per second,[6] while 1 meter per second is a safe speed for a child's tricycle. An archer's arrow can fly at about 100 meters per second,[7] while 1 meter per second is about the speed a lost feather from a diving peregrine falcon floats to the ground.

With increased speed comes greater density. Yes, you read right. Teenagers really are brain dense, and as many parents suspect, they grow more so with each passing day. Thanks to the miracle of magnetic resonance imaging (MRI scans), we can clearly see the brains of kids actually become more dense as they enter adolescence. Believe it or not, this is a good thing. Today's neuroscience reveals that though the brain's gray matter volume in adolescents tends to be lower than in young children, the amount of gray matter in their heads is packed in much more tightly.[8] As their brains develop over the adolescent years, they will eventually reach about 40 percent white matter by adulthood. In the meantime, young brains offer up 86 billion nerve cells, forming some 60 trillion chatty synaptic connections that still require a lot of sheer pruning and protective coating.

Usually at this point the parents of teens are reading along, thinking something like, *There must have been a labor shortage of master gardeners and certified electricians when my child was infected with adolescence. It feels more like an overcaffeinated Edward Scissorhands is wildly shearing away at the synaptic connections inside my kid's thick skull. Everything I say seems to go in one ear and out the other, without much getting in the way.*

Despite how it may sound, and contrary to the principle of causation, synaptic pruning does not provide an explanation for why parents worldwide and throughout history believe that most teens have lost their dense minds. In fact, quite the opposite is happening. The neural connection edits in the teenage brain are totally natural and a very important stage of adolescent brain development. What comes of pruning away billions of unused and inefficient neural pathways while simultaneously protecting and supercharging billions more is called *neuroplasticity*. Basically, neuroplasticity is brain sculpting, mind molding, and the ability to adjust one's thinking. So take a deep breath and marvel in the miracle that your kid's brain is undergoing a massive renovation to become more efficient, open, and mentally mature. Slowly, over time.

We Know What You Are Thinking

Before we get into how your child's growing brain's mindset is influenced by different parenting styles, let's address a common concern many parents spend a great deal of time thinking about:

Are we doing the right things, at the right time, to fully prepare our kids for _____?

Only you can fill in the blank. The most popular scenarios include day care, kindergarten, overnight camp, middle school, dating, high school, driving, college, and life on their own. If any of these considerations have crossed your mind, you can rest assured that you are in good company. In fact, you stand in the thick of a very large crowd. Ask around and you'll find most parents' concerns about their kids' readiness only seem to intensify as they get older. According to the C. S. Mott Children's Hospital National Poll on Children's Health at the University of Michigan, the majority of parents say that when it comes to preparing their children for adulthood, they would give low ranking for their kid's ability to handle basic tasks. Though 97 percent of parents report they are helping their teen become more independent, 60 percent say their child lacks the maturity, time, and know-how to take on more responsibility.[9]

Adding to our child-rearing concerns is the near universal desire parents possess to see into the future of their kids. Like most good parents, you too want your children to grow up to enjoy a life that is better than your own. This makes it only natural to want some kind of prediction, a quick vision, just a little glimpse of the level of "success" you hope they will enjoy in the years to come. Knowing it's best to steer clear of shady soothsayers and cloudy crystal balls, parents tend to lean heavily into more tangible forecasts of their child's potential for greatness. The most popular measures are of course their academic performance, the size and number of trophies and awards, and the quantity and quality of the company they keep. Unfortunately, each serves as little more than a placebo for parental anxiety when compared to the biggest and most powerful predictor of our kid's future success: their environment.

Now before you think we just took a hard left turn into a discussion about the biodiversity of complex ecosystems in today's Anthropocene period, you can relax. We'll leave that up to you and your child in a late-night makeup science homework marathon yet to come. We're still on the topic of raising kids ready. Unfortunately, this doesn't make the discussion any less complicated at times. That's because, in the case of predicting most children's potential for future achievements, the chance of "making it" depends a great deal on their access to environments that nurture and promote success.[10] Maybe this sounds like a no-brainer, but that hasn't always been the case in the prove-it-or-lose-it circles of social scientists. Turns out that after decades of debate about nature vs. nurture, researchers have finally announced a winner. The clear champion in the development of our kids' skills, abilities, and access to socioeconomic mobility is . . . NURTURE.

Regrettably, not all nurturing is equal. Whereas money can't buy happiness, affluence can afford better schools, needed tutors, more experienced coaches, and access to exclusive invitation-only social events. Basically, wealthier families have greater means to material supports and social advantages than the poor and even average-income families. That's probably not what you were hoping to read. It doesn't feel right to hear once again that when disadvantaged and under-resourced children succeed in life, they often do so in spite of their environment, while affluent kids are protected and propelled ahead because their families can afford the best of environments. It's not fair that a family's prosperity would be a stronger indicator of a child's future success than intelligence, talent, or commitment to the secret ingredient of making any dream come true—hard work.

But wait, that's not all. Didn't we already agree that parenting is hard work? We did, and good thing too. Because it turns out there is a secret ingredient within the environment in which we nurture our kids that *outperforms* monetary affluence. This means there is great hope for parents who wish to see their children thrive in any environment, no matter their financial status. Drum roll, please. The most powerful influence on your child developing a positive mindset and confident willingness to try new things is . . . wait for it . . . *YOU*. That's right, it's you. The parent. Specifically, *how* you parent. Also commonly and professionally called your parenting style.

Parenting Styles

To better understand how the mindsets of our children are influenced by our parenting styles, we have committed the next few pages to a crash course in the four child-rearing techniques most commonly recognized by developmental psychologists worldwide.

First researched in the 1960s by psychologist Diana Baumrind at the University of California–Berkeley and later expanded upon by Stanford University researchers Eleanor Maccoby and John Martin, there are four prominent parental behavior types. Each has been studied and scrutinized by understandably protective parents and reputation-sensitive psychologists alike for years. As parents we should find the consistency of their research findings reassuring. The work of psychologists Baumrind, Maccoby, and Martin is sound, well respected, and recognized in the exacting world of developmental psychologists as definitive.

Of the four types of parenting, one raises confident and capable kids far better than the other three. To clearly distinguish the superior parenting style, we must first identify two fundamental and familiar parenting behaviors. They are simply how *demanding* we are as parents and how *responsive* we are to our kids. Recognizing that people hold varying interpretations of these terms, let's agree to describe *demanding* as the level to which a parent more (+) or less (−) communicates and enforces behavioral expectations with a child. We will define *responsive* as the degree to which a parent more (+) or less (−) responds to their child's needs. By assessing more (+) or less (−) demanding and more (+) or less (−) responsive, we can separate each unique approach to child-rearing into a four quadrant framework we'll call parenting styles.

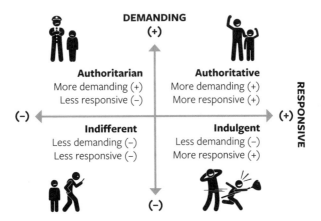

To spare us time and energy, here are some simple descriptions and brief examples of the four different parenting styles. We will start with the three that have proven to not work well in fostering confident and capable children and conclude with the only one that does. Spoiler alert: Authoritative parenting wins hands down.

Indifferent: *"I don't care. Do whatever you want."*

(−) Less Demanding
(−) Less Responsive

Indifferent parents just don't seem to give a . . . You might hear them say something about their responsibilities as a parent like, "The kids will be fine. They're not really hurting anything," or "As far as I'm concerned, let them do what they want. You know they are going to find a way to do it anyway." By permitting their children to do and be as they please, indifferent parents take the easy way out, by checking out. They are quick to disengage from any unwanted responsibilities that come with raising children. A lack of supervision and very few behavioral instructions keep the time and inconvenience they must commit to parenting to a bare minimum. Communication of all types tends to be low, discipline is soft, and expectations are few. Without clear guidelines, their child has little to no accountability for bad behavior, due to a lack of parental follow-through. Basically, Indifferent parents will eventually be described by their children as, "Yah, so, my parents weren't really there much for me while I was growing up."

- An *Indifferent parent* permits their children to do and be as they please.

Indulgent: *"Sure thing, sweetie. We'll do whatever you want."*

(–) Less Demanding

(+) More Responsive

Indulgent parents do just as the name suggests. They indulge their children.

This is also known as spoiling your kids. Sometimes rotten. In an attempt to avoid the potential pain of conflict and to gain the favor of their children, Indulgent parents put their child's needs and wants first—in an unhealthy way. They often sacrifice discipline for approval and potential conflict for peace.

Indulgent parents might say, "Look. Kids have enough to deal with these days. I just don't see the need for my child to take on any additional stress. Not when there's something I can do about it." From a surface-level view, this might seem understandable, considering stress is one of the leading causes of poor performance in children. Though each of us reacts to stressful situations differently,[11] stress in children can stem from their perception that they are incapable of coping with the demands placed on them or in situations they interpret to be a threat to their personal well-being.[12]

So sure, any good parent should step in to support and protect their child from the demands of life. Shouldn't they?

Yes and no. If on occasion we do things for our kids because we are showing them love and kindness, then yes. But if by hovering around, always ready to step in to "deal" with the situation, an Indulgent parent consistently does for their children what they could and should learn to do for themselves, then no. No, because repeatedly indulging their child in this way can keep them from gaining the practical experience and depth of independence they need to succeed. Both in the moment and in the future. This is why indulged children often remain dependent on their parents longer. When faced with normal, everyday demands, they can feel unequipped and, while addressing the true trials of life, totally unprepared.

- An *Indulgent parent* does for their children what their children could and should learn to do for themselves.

Authoritarian: *"You'll do it because I said so. That's why!"*

(+) More Demanding
(−) Less Responsive

Let's just say it. *Authoritarian parents* are also called drill sergeant parents. At least that's the gossip between neighbors and definitely how their children describe them to friends. Like a stiff-necked drill instructor training young recruits, an authoritarian parent's commands are expected to be carried out as ordered. Respect and discipline are essential and often enforced with plenty of tough love, strict punishment, and little empathy. In an attempt to toughen up kids, Authoritarian parenting tends to be an adult-centered, top-down, leader-over-followers type of parenting that focuses more on rules than relationships. Communication is often a narrow one-way street that holds little room for the display of unnecessary emotions. What really matters is that the child understands that the parent knows what's best. So they had *better* get with the program. Because as long as they live under this roof, "It's my way or the highway."

• An *Authoritarian parent* demands respect, and their commands are expected to be carried out as ordered.

Authoritative: *"I know that you can do this. Here's why."*

(+) More Demanding
(+) More Responsive

Authoritative parents could be considered the five-star rating of parenting styles. Like most of their best-in-class performers, Authoritative parents really are in a league of their own. Authoritative parenting is hard work that requires dedication to the thoughtful balancing act of parenting with firm expectations and boundaries alongside loving care and responsiveness consistent and specific to the needs of each child.

Authoritative parents provide stability through nurturing, engaging, and empathizing with their children. By doing so, they can also successfully set behavior rules that are cast in stone, establish clearly defined and explained restrictions, and provide needed discipline that nurtures self-discipline and autonomy in your children. This type of parenting with proactive purpose rather than reactive responses has yielded impressive results: children of authoritative parents measure the most motivated, most competent, and most achievement oriented.[13] And that's just for starters. Much to the pleasure of parents, children, and educators in schools worldwide, the authoritative parenting style includes clear associations with positive academic performances. Unfortunately, the opposite is also true. Bossy authoritarian parenting and those more permissive parenting styles hold negative associations with student grades.[14]

SET

Authoritative parenting is all about building high levels of trust with children through nurturing, engagement, reasoning, empathy, and self-discipline. In turn, the authoritative parenting style helps children develop intrinsic motivation (doing an activity for itself and the pleasure and satisfaction derived from participating) and intrinsic goals.[15] And the positive benefits of an authoritative parenting style remain even after "adulting" children graduate from high school and leave home for college. "Parenting characteristics such as supportiveness and warmth continue to play an important role in influencing a student's academic performance even after entering college."[16]

- An *Authoritative parent* thoughtfully balances their parenting with clear, firm expectations and boundaries alongside loving care and responsiveness consistent and specific to the needs of each child.

Captain Obvious

It doesn't take a genius to see that when it comes to parenting styles, Authoritative wins hands down. The bad news is, this kind of parenting isn't easy. It requires purpose, practice, and patience. The good news is, purpose, practice, and patience are all beneficial to both parents and kids, no matter what stage of life you are in.

To parent with purpose is an awesome task. Bringing our kids up in ways that when they are grown, they are both confident and capable should give us a great sense of resolve and determination. It should give us a real since of purpose. Practicing ways to parent with purpose means we will get better at raising our kids, a little at a time. So be patient with yourself.

Interestingly, of all the significant aspects of what makes Authoritative parenting work, the one we get asked about regularly is what exactly defines a kid's "needs." Well, legally speaking, the standards are very low. Parents are only required to supply their minor child with food, clothing, shelter, and basic care. So long as they receive adequate nutrition, wear appropriate coverings, have a roof over their head, and see a doctor every now and then, that will do. Unfortunately, this is not a joke.

Thankfully, when good parents pose the question about kids' true needs, they aren't asking us to define the very least they must provide. Instead, most are looking for guidance on how to keep the bar from being raised too high by unrealistic influencers who intrude upon and sway their kid's expectations of needs versus wants.

So what are your kids' true "needs"? Without question they need to be safe. They need to be loved. They need to belong. Listen carefully and kids will tell you this is also what they want most. Maybe not in those exact words. But yes, that's what they truly need and want. Still, most parents say all they hear their kids complain about is that they need more *stuff*.

Ask our sons and they'll both say we regularly reminded them that all their required "needs" for more stuff have been met. And exceeded. Their requests for things like the latest and greatest video game download, pair of collector sneakers, upgraded phone, or new car fall far outside our legal parenting obligations. Love and kindness we have always shared with them beyond measure and without conditions, like we are relational bazillionaires. But as for the stuff they mistakenly called "needs," there are limits.

When it comes to ways we can help equip them with the skillsets and toolsets required to develop their confidence and capabilities, we'd be happy to contribute. How they use those skills and tools is up to them. It's our hope and prayer that with the mindset of confidence, they'll be willing to see life's many demands as challenges. Of course, they will also need the skillsets and toolsets that make such challenges opportunities to thrive. We can only believe you desire the same for your kids too.

No Hovering

We are regularly shocked by memes, posts, and articles that attempt to justify some very bad parental behavior. On the basis that the world is a dangerous and unpredictable place, many parents have taken the job of protecting their children way too far. There's no pressure, stress, or rival that will keep this kind of unapologetic parent from deflecting their kid's daily dangers like the overwatchful, overinvolved, and overreaching "nurturer" who knows best. Also known as cosseting, lawn mower, snowplow, and bulldozer parents, the more common title given to those who control and clear the way for their kids is *helicopter parents*. Call them what you like, the truth is, hovering around and swooping in when kids encounter trouble can inflict far more harm on a child than provide help for them.

Helicopter Parents

In his 1969 book *Parents & Teenagers*, bestselling author, educator, child psychologist, and parent Dr. Haim Ginott was the first to introduce the world to the term *helicopter parents*.[17] Dr. Ginott based the term on how the teens he worked with described their extreme annoyance with their parents' consistent "hovering" over them.[18] Under the watchful eye of ever-present and constantly aware helicopter parents, they were rarely allowed to make mistakes or feel the pain of failure. These 1960s kids grew up, became parents themselves, and repeated the overparenting practice of swooping in to support or quickly whisk their child away to safety. The same was done with kids in the 1970s, '80s, and '90s, and as we all know, the next generation of twenty-first-century helicopter parents is probably the worst yet.

Different than engaged parents, today's helicopter parents grab hold of their child's perceived well-being with an unhealthy vice-tight grip. Overcontrolling, overprotecting, and overfocused on overperfecting their kids, helicopter parents can't let go of believing they know what's right—and wrong—for their child. Thinking back to our previous discussion about the four parenting styles, such practices can land helicopter parents squarely in either the dreaded Authoritarian or the permissive Indulgent parenting styles. Honestly believing they know what's best for their child, Authoritarian helicopter parents are committed to deciding the present and future steps their kids will take, without demonstrating and teaching their children the adequate skills they need to develop for themselves true maturity and independence.[19] Indulgent parents do the same by ensuring their kid gets what they want without the expectation of them needing to work for it. Strict or lax, both Authoritarian and Indulgent styles of helicopter parenting provide few opportunities for kids to learn how to fend for themselves.

So why do some parents believe it's necessary to protectively hang all over their kids? Does the cause stem from their kid's needs, or the parent's? The answer can become both. Like a riddle that goes round and round trying to determine which came first, the chicken or the egg, the underlying reason helicopter parents feel it's necessary for them to hover stems from their desire to keep their kids from having to experience the negative outcomes associated with the demands of life.[20] These are the very same outcomes the Readiness Assessment predicts of kids who rate as Not Ready. Unwilling or unable to face the urgent requests or specific efforts of everyday life can leave helicopter-supported kids feeling threatened rather than challenged by life. They often perform poorly rather than positively and slip into enduring, remaining as is, and simply existing behaviors of survival rather than thriving in the growth and prosperity of success. No parent wants that for their child. But instead of empowering their kids, helicopter parents over flex their control muscles in an attempt to protect their own from possible "harm" before any real damage can be done. But in order to foresee and potentially intervene in any such danger, they must constantly be hovering overhead.

In young children, tweens, and teens, the effect of helicopter parenting can lead to some very bad outcomes. The consequences can include greater degrees of negative internalizing behaviors in kids, such as stress, anxiety, and depression.[21] In young adults, hovering parenting practices are directly related to greater levels of neuroticism, less willingness to experience new things, increased dependency, and reduced psychological well-being.[22] None of these physical, social, or psychological behaviors help kids become more ready for life on their own. The fact is, helicopter parenting can produce the exact opposite results of what the parents are attempting to achieve.

Unfortunately, the flight pattern for whirlybird parenting is usually a dangerously congested airspace. Ask any schoolteacher or sports coach what the most difficult aspects of their job are and they'll place dealing with helicopter parents near the top of their list.

Here's an all-too-familiar example that led to a creative plea from one sports coach. Fed up with parents who are convinced that their kid deserves to only experience the thrill of victory and never the agony of defeat, a full-time math teacher, part-time baseball coach had custom signs made and hung on the fences facing both the home team and the visitor bleachers.

No surprise, he caught some heavy flak from a few insulted folks. They viewed the sign as a snide insinuation that parents don't know as much about sports as coaches. No one should be allowed to tell them they can't spend the entire game shouting play directions at their kids. How dare the school suggest that's the coach's job.

Drone Parents

As bad as helicopter parenting sounds, believe it or not, it gets worse. Some helicopter parents have upgraded their hovering abilities with advanced tactics that grant them even greater operational control over their kids. Feared and loathed by university professors, athletic coaches, bank managers, employers, and landlords everywhere, the next generation of whirlwind-producing parents have unfortunately earned their very daunting nickname: drone parents.

Where helicopter parents are known for constantly hovering over their kids, swooping in to drop supplies, give directions, or provide rescue, drone parents utilize far more stealth-like tactics to control their kids. Not so obviously seen or heard as their low-flying predecessors, drone parents use the advantage of technology to run surveillance, gather intel, and strike at targets they deem threatening to their child's well-being. They infiltrate their kid's lives in ways that manipulate and manage their child's behavior, experiences, and personal liabilities. Without permission, and often in secret, they monitor social media accounts, cell phone usage, GPS locations, bank account activity, grades at school, and even their kid's work schedule.

Depending on the age and maturity of your child, none of these activities are individually bad in and of themselves. Considering most families share cell and data plans, video streaming subscriptions, insurance policies, and banking services, it's perfectly normal for parents to occasionally get a digital glimpse into their kid's life. Cars come equipped with navigation systems that sync with phone apps, schools expect students and parents to regularly access their shared online portals, and linking bank accounts makes it easy to transfer funds to and from different family members. Let's face it, there's an app, login, subscription, and alert for about everything your kid does today. But some parents use their excess access to information to do far more than keep an eye on things. Drone parents covertly gather intel on their kids, dirt on their "questionable" friends, and target perceived threats that they interpret as getting in the way of their kid's best interests.

We first heard about the attack tactics of drone parents following a speaking engagement at a large state university. After delivering a keynote on the importance of stewardship in leadership, the administration hosted a reception that included some informal Q&A time with the speaker. One of the university professors asked for advice on how to combat future drone parent strikes. With obvious angst, they explained how unhappy students engage their parents to strike back at faculty whom the student feels have done them wrong. Like a class they hoped to register for was full and the professor wouldn't open just *one* additional seat for them. Maybe a coach didn't give them a starting position even though they are *obviously* better than the other players. Perhaps the director of student housing assigned the dorm room they *really* wanted to someone else. Whatever the reason for their displeasure, students were often bringing their complaints to a parent, rather than the university. In response, drone parents would do their research, draft a plan, and launch an attack. From a safe distance, they make phone calls, write emails, and post online in an attempt to fix things for their kid and do some damage to the university at the same time. And drone parents know where and how to strike. They hit fast, hard, and with seemingly little regard for the potential harm they might inflict on faculty, either personally or professionally.

In one such drone parent attack, a dean answered a blistering phone call from an enraged parent about a grade their child received on their first ever college paper. Apparently, back in high school, the student had gotten nothing but straight A's on all their writing assignments. So certainly their college professor had made a mistake in grading the paper. That or they singled their child out, purposefully gave them a low grade, and were looking to make an example of them before the entire class. Whatever the reason, the parent demanded the grade be changed to an A. They also insisted the dean take immediate disciplinary action against the professor. If they didn't, the drone parent threatened to stop making financial contributions to the school's alumni fundraising efforts. That and their child would be transferring to a better, more prestigious school.

If we were to choose one word to describe how drone parents act, it would be invasive. Able to infiltrate, drone parents violate the autonomy their kids need to make decisions and resolve issues on their own.

Stay Grounded

What we are about to share with you may come as a shock to some parents. So please take a few calming breaths before reading the conclusion of this chapter.

Your kid is not going to be good at everything. They do not deserve a trophy for simply participating, or for that matter, anything beyond the polished bronze of third place. Believe it or not, their ego can handle not always winning, and one day they will thank you for teaching them to be resilient. Because resilient people can weather, recover, and bounce forward following disappointments, difficulties, and failures, and all three are an unavoidable part of life. IRL.

Notice that we said bounce forward, not bounce back. Kids who develop a can-do, self-efficacy, growth mindset from supportive Authoritative parents are the kind of kids who, after not always winning, still stand with their feet on solid ground *and* their head in the clouds.

What empowers resilient kids to stay grounded while envisioning the best future imaginable is their combined willingness and ability to navigate through life's many demands. Whereas hovering parents stifle the development of such qualities in their kids by directing and redirecting them away from the same demands of life because they are interpreted as threats to survive.

Any message we give our kids other than some people excel because they are better prepared—more willing and able—is an inaccurate and potentially dangerous lie to tell our kids. Instead of placebo trophies for everyone, give your kids words of encouragement, high-fives, and hugs when they do their best. That and stop for ice cream after the game, recital, concert, race, or performance, not as a reward, but because it's a family tradition. Win or lose.

5. SKILLSET

skill·set

noun

A particular combination of skills that a person has developed, especially ones that can be used to perform a specific task or set of tasks needed to do a job.

#winning

It's one thing for your child to learn how to do a few simple daily tasks on their own, like feeding a pet, loading the dishwasher, or putting their shoes away. It's a completely different challenge to raise them in a way that intentionally provides opportunities for them to learn the vast and diverse set of skills they'll need to handle almost any demand they'll face in life. Just spend a few minutes scrolling the abyss of social media posts created by young people in their coming-of-age years and you're sure to be flooded with content that makes the point abundantly clear. Whether or not they know it, many of their posts reveal a great deal about who's thriving and who's surviving in their skillset development.

Picture this. A social media post featuring a typical task completed by most adults on most every day of the week. Like making a bed, preparing a meal, or folding clothes. What's untypical about some of these tweets, status updates, reels, stories, pins, videos, images, and posts is that they often include the hashtag caption #*winning*.

> Made my bed this morning #*winning*. Dinner at home to-
> night #*winning*. Laundry day #*winning*.

If the same images were shared with the world by an exhausted parent who had once again worked all day; shuttled the kids between sports practice, music lessons, and a dance recital; took the dog to the vet; and somehow managed to squeeze in a run to the grocery store, then yes, #winning would be an accurate statement worth sharing. Maybe even an understatement. But when the post comes from a single and available twenty-two-year-old, working part time, who is living their #bestlife in a corner condo with water views from their chef's kitchen's wall of windows, most normal people might think their well-lit, soft-filtered #winning post should really be labeled #playing.

The truth of the matter is, the broad skillset kids need to move past #playing with #standard achievements to make #winning over the daily demands of life a #normal thing can take years to build. Skills are simply not that #casual and are seldom come by in one-and-done experiences. Technically speaking, skills are the mechanics that enable a person to perform well consistently. Individually, the seemingly little life skills we use daily feel insignificant and are seldom celebrated. That's because on their own, many of them just aren't that impressive. But added together with other skills and the accumulation of all the little abilities your kid practices, these become the vast skillset they can use to make a difference in both their life and in the lives of others.

True, it's a long way between your kids learning how to do simple tasks, like straightening, tucking, and folding the bedsheets in the morning, and learning how to handle far more significant demands in ways that grant them access to life-defining opportunities. But we all have to start somewhere.

"If you want to change the world, start off by making your bed"[1] was the wise advice shared with over 8,000 graduates by retired United States Navy four-star admiral William McRaven. In his university-wide commencement speech delivered to the University of Texas, the decorated Navy SEAL, ninth commander of the US Special Operations Command, and father of three shared ten lessons for overcoming struggles in a way that changes ourselves and the world around us.[2] Top of his list, start each day by making your bed.

> If you make your bed every morning you will have accomplished the first task of the day. It will give you a small sense of pride, and it will encourage you to do another task and another and another. By the end of the day, that one task completed will have turned into many tasks completed. Making your bed will also reinforce the fact that little things in life matter. If you can't do the little things right, you will never do the big things right.
>
> And, if by chance you have a miserable day, you will come home to a bed that is made—that you made—and a made bed gives you encouragement that tomorrow will be better.
>
> If you want to change the world, start off by making your bed.[3]

Two things stand out in this short segment of Admiral McRaven's speech. First, there are a lot of tasks that need to be done each day. *"By the end of the day, that one task completed will have turned into many tasks completed."* And second, just how much the little things matter. *"Making your bed will also reinforce the fact that little things in life matter. If you can't do the little things right, you will never do the big things right."*

So very true. Where most kids may only face a couple "big things" each day, a steady stream of little things always seems to pop up around them. In fact, when added up at the end of the day, the total number of little things that place demands on their time and attention might shock you. Where experts in personal and professional organization suggest not taking on more than three big to-do tasks per day, there are still hundreds of little responsibilities that come between making the bed in the morning and messing it back up again at night. Those who manage to accomplish a few big goals daily know the secret to success lies in doing the little things right. Doing little things right makes big things possible.

Mature people with a sizable collection of life skills see the constant flow of little tasks as manageable and routine—the kind of stuff that just needs to get done each day. In a way, this makes them master taskers. No, not taskmasters. A *taskmaster* is a person who imposes a harsh or difficult workload on someone else. Taskmasters are quite the opposite of master taskers. *Master taskers* possess a healthy skillset of what's required to do a little of this, some of that, and a bunch of other things. Both small and large.

On the opposite end of the ability spectrum are the people who lack the basic skills needed to handle the expected and unexpected tasks of life. What others consider usual or mundane little challenges, the unskilled see as obstacles. They view them as threats. Sometimes big ones. Remember the Readiness Assessment? When your child is both willing (Mindset) and able (Skillset + Toolset) to take on a demand, the task becomes a challenge. And our brains thrive on challenges. Yet if a kid's abilities are found wanting—in this case lacking the specific skillset needed to perform a task— they can feel threatened. And our brains will do just about anything to avoid or survive a threat.

A funny and innocent example of doing the little things right to make the big things possible happened to the classmate of a friend's son early in his first year away at college. We have told the story more than a few times and have even given the episode a name. We call it "Rocket Science and Laundry Machines."

Rocket Science and Laundry Machines

A close friend's son attends one of the most prestigious aeronautical universities in the world. There isn't a course load too heavy, study too difficult, or aspiration too far out of reach for these future engineers, aviators, and rocket scientists. That is, until it comes to doing laundry.

In a plea for help, the son's classmate texted his mom from school.

> SOMETHING IS WRONG

> I NEED HELP

Concerned for his well-being, the mother stopped everything and replied immediately. Much to her relief, her son was safe and the problem was far from life threatening. Instead, she had to laugh to herself when she learned the issue had to do with the dorm's laundry machines. His clothes weren't getting clean. They didn't smell right, feel right, or come out stain free like they did when Mom did his wash. Knowing she had sent her son to school with the same detergent pods they used at home, she texted back asking how exactly he was doing his laundry.

> **Son**
> i know how mom

> **Mom**
> Humor me. Walk me through it.

> **Son**
> i put my clothes in the machine
>
> pick the kind of wash
>
> put a pod in the slot
>
> close the door

press start

Mom
Where do you put the pod?

Son
in the slot

Mom
What slot?

Son
the one on top

Mom
You don't put the pod in with the clothes?

Son
why would I do that

Mom
How is the slot labeled? Go check.

Son
? now ?

Mom
Yes now.

Text me when you find out what the slot is for.

Five minutes later . . .

Son
bleach

my bad

love you mom

84

Like we said, the story is an innocent example of how getting the seemingly little things right can be difficult the first few times. It's also a far-too-common reality for many kids who should know better by their age. Similar stories can be told by dorm resident advisors, campus life coordinators, mentors, and teachers offering Life Skills 101 classes. In addition to their studies, work schedule, and a busy social life, many newly independent kids are also having to learn the hard way how to do for themselves what they could and should have been doing for years.

So what are the best ways for kids to learn to tackle the tasks of life for themselves? Before they strike out on their own? The answer might be more familiar than most parents think. After all, what worked for us when we were their age might actually be worth repeating.

What a Chore

We hear a lot from parents about their kids doing chores. Rather, a lot of parents talk about how difficult it can be to get their kids to *do* their chores. If you are feeling the same, please rest assured, you are not alone. But you are in the minority. That's because fewer and fewer parents are holding true to the age-old expectation that kids should do their part to help out around the house.

Today, only about 28 percent of parents require their children to do chores. Any chores. That number seems shockingly low considering the same parents who don't expect their twenty-first-century kids to contribute were expected to chip in when they were young. Some 82 percent of current parents report they were taught how to and were expected to help clean, wash, mow, cook, empty the trash, run errands, and watch their younger siblings when they were growing up.[4] Some even did all that work without pay. What they received as an "allowance" was earned by doing more than what was expected of them in their daily chores.

For kids today in the nearly three-quarters of homes where they aren't asked to do anything around the house, the chores their parents did back in the day may sound like a form of child labor. Yet decades of research clearly shows that kids who had regular chores in the home fared far better later in life than kids who didn't.[5] Turns out, sparing children from performing even the most basic of household tasks can spoil their future selves. In fact, chores were the best predictor of which kids were more likely to become happy, healthy, independent adults.[6] Turns out a little division of labor around the home goes a long way.

Fair Share

Most parents have a few good stories, and a couple of really bad ones, about battling with their children over doing chores. We have our fair share of both. Our kids were taught to take care of their own rooms, bathrooms, and laundry when they were young. If they wanted a late breakfast, snack, or "linner" (that's what we called their teenage meal between lunch and dinner), they knew how to open the refrigerator and find their way around the kitchen. They learned how to use a vacuum, dishwasher, shovel, paint-brush, and pressure washer as soon as their hand-eye coordination allowed.

For their efforts, they received shares. Shares were our family's version of an allowance. We didn't particularly like the term *allowance* because it sounded a bit too entitled for our tastes. Just because they are our kids, live in our home, and helped to clean up what they messed up, why should they get paid? We didn't feel like birthright gave them any *allowance* to an expected weekly cash income. Instead, if they did their share to help out and keep our home profitable, they could earn a portion of the home's profits.

Much like shareholders in a business receive a return on their investment, our kids received a share of what remained after all the monthly bills were paid. The more they did to support our home and reduce expenses, the more profit we could all enjoy. Close the back door and the air conditioner doesn't drive the electric bill up. Take reasonable-length showers, the gas and water bills stay reasonable. Turn the lights off when leaving a room, put the milk away, and don't leave your jacket on the bus. You get the idea. They did too. In addition to doing the everyday stuff that kept our home going, they committed to help keep our expenses down and our budget manageable. For that, they received shares of between $0.00 and $20.00 a week.

Bidding War

When our son Cole was about thirteen, he made up his mind that it was time to start earning more money than his family shares brought in each week. His older brother had recently started his first job, and the large paychecks he deposited in the bank looked pretty good to Cole. Much to Cole's frustration, his young age made his job prospects few and far between in our suburban community. That is, until he learned what our neighbors were paying to have their lawns professionally mowed each week. At twenty-five dollars per zone, he figured he was living in the middle of a green-grass-growing gold mine.

After knocking on a few doors, though, Cole returned home with no new clients, zero leads, and next to nothing that he could do to change his low cash-flow situation. He had encountered his first challenge as a young businessperson. Competition. The big professional yard care companies had a tight hold on almost every lawn in the neighborhood. All our neighbors were locked into seasonal contracts and nobody was hiring. Disappointed and discouraged, he sat in the garage, frustrated that it looked like he might be going out of business before he even got started.

Not willing to give in so easily, he strategized on how to approach the one remaining home that might just hire him. The owners were real sticklers about mowing their own grass and prided themselves in working together each weekend to do all their own yardwork. It just so happens Cole knew the family pretty well. Well enough to call two of them his parents.

Cole's first proposal was a good one. By him taking over the regular mowing, we could focus more of our time on checking off other items on our weekend to-do list. He was even willing to offer his services at the exclusive friends-and-family discounted price of only twenty dollars per zone. Impressed by his entrepreneurial spirit and wanting to make a deposit in our relationship account, we made Cole a counteroffer. Ten dollars. Knowing Cole was born a natural negotiator, we completely expected him to come back with a strong counteroffer. And he did. After going back and forth a few times, we hammered out the details and settled at fifteen dollars for both front and back yard mows and an extra five for edging. Depending on growth and weather conditions, he could mow twice a week and we would pay in cash.

The deal only lasted a few summers before Cole got his driver's license and a more regular job at a local pizza place. His new boss loved him as an employee. He arrived on time, worked hard, and stayed till the job was done, and done right. As parents, we were proud to hear the restaurant owners tell us how much they valued having to teach Cole only about pizza and not how to be a good worker and reliable employee. With his strong work ethic and dedication to excellence, he persuaded his boss he was worth a full dollar-an-hour raise. As he likes to say when depositing his paychecks, "That's money in the bank."

Life Skills 101

Better late than never. This once sarcastic statement has become a familiar mantra for many newly minted young adults. Scrambling to learn the necessary life skills required to truly cut the cord of dependence on their parents, more teens and twentysomethings are finding it necessary to finally learn how to do many of life's seemingly basics tasks on their own. For the first time.

So many young people are falling behind in their can-do abilities that many colleges and universities have added "adulting" courses to their catalog of classes. Within the pursuit of a degree, students can also attend courses where the syllabus exclusively focuses on the teaching of essential life skills, 101. Curriculum includes the theory and practices of effective communication, relationship health, stress management, and financial literacy—all are very important interpersonal soft skills to grasp, yet prove to be only part of what many students failed to learn prior to graduating high school. So, hard skills lessons are added to cover the daily basics, like how to do laundry, cook meals, manage time, and even ways to practice better health and personal hygiene. Just for starters. Keep in mind the students enrolled in these courses are some of the same kids who earned the highest scores on their college-entrance SAT, ACT, and AP tests. Yet they struggle to fry an egg, iron a shirt, or fill out a job application. Once again, how does the saying go? *Better late than never.*

Get a Job

Not surprisingly, research shows a strong link between life skills know-how and college graduates landing degree-worthy work. Employment studies cite as much as 45 percent of recent graduates find themselves *under*employed.[7] Basically, many college grads with mountains of school debt are taking low-paying jobs that do not require their degree. But why?

Such poor employment outcomes may be the result of young adults entering the workforce unprepared for the full breadth and depth of the task at hand. Yes, they have the education needed to get hired and perform the entry-level hard skills required of the job, yet many lack the sustainable soft skills and life skills needed to keep the job, let alone get what they really want—to be promoted.[8]

Some of the most important skills for recent college graduates to master include oral and written communication, critical thinking, ethical judgment and decision-making, working effectively in teams, working independently, self-motivation, and applying their knowledge and skills in real-world settings. Hiring managers and business executives agree that the level of stewardship required to break in and to remain valuable in the workplace today is not easily managed by beginners. Those who demonstrate the greatest level of workforce readiness also prove themselves to be self-disciplined, self-confident, responsible, independent, and mature in practicing their essential personal life skills.[9] In other words, they can handle their work life because they know how to handle their personal life.

The need to effectively balance and manage the demands of work and life brings us back full circle to why colleges and universities are offering courses in basic life skills readiness. It's an unwritten win-win agreement as employers seek high-achieving workforce-ready hires, and universities producing the most employable graduates are often rated the highest by industry leaders. So, the graduates who are most likely to gain and retain employment are those who have practiced and proven they possess the hard *and* soft skills needed to succeed both on *and* off the job.

How you introduce your child to learning and practicing the skills needed to succeed on their own is your decision. Some families are committed to preparing their kids a little at a time over the years. Others try to cram in as many lessons as possible in the short time remaining before their kids strike out on their own. Though intentions are good, rarely does the "catch up if you can" method go as planned. More often than not, waiting until the last minute creates unnecessary friction and unwelcome conflict between now-feral teens and their past-frustrated parents.

Then there are the parents who have no plan at all. Perhaps sending their kids off to school or out into the world on their own is the plan. As we previously mentioned, college Life Skills

101 courses or enrolling in the school of hard knocks may be the "better late than never" option, but it can also easily become the "too little, too late" reason that kids who are old enough to know better find themselves experiencing very real difficulties in adulting.

6. PHASES AND STAGES

Scaffolding

Think about the role you play in guiding your child as they develop their skillset abilities like you are building a protective structure around them. Not like some impenetrable shield to safeguard them from the world. More like the temporary scaffolding you see on a construction jobsite.

Similar to how the web of platforms grants laborers access to various levels of work, the concept of building scaffolding around your kids allows you to layer their learning through the developmental stages of their young life. From the ground up, the sound support of scaffolding will assist your child in safely accessing heights in their personal development that otherwise would be difficult to reach.

Not to be confused with a ladder that can provide a straight climb to the top, scaffolding is used to assist in the construction of broad and often long-term builds. The assembly of your child's abilities will require years of layering and is best done in developmentally and environmentally appropriate stages. The good news is, most parents use some degree of scaffolding naturally when it comes to assisting our children in mastering the many skills introduced throughout the multiple phases of their pre-adult life. Problems arise when parents introduce new skills too early or push their children to rank up faster and higher than they should go at that time.

The purpose of scaffolding around your child is not to prop them up or to give them a more impressive climb to the top than what the other kids' parents can provide. Neither is scaffolding intended to entitle children to freely do whatever, wherever they want on the biggest virtual jungle gym playset imaginable. The goal of scaffolding is to provide our kids with temporary support that will later be removed as they learn and practice the character and life skills they'll need to one day stand tall on their own.

Again, most parents instinctively provide some degree of scaffolding around their kids. While intuitive support is good, knowing specifically when and to what degree structure is needed makes it even better. Consciously guiding your child in discovering, attempting, and practicing the abilities they will need to succeed can be divided into three unique learning phases.

Phase 1: Passive Learning

Phase 2: Active Learning

Phase 3: Applied Learning

Think of the three phases as a progression. They are not strictly bound by age, yet the developmental stages your child has already aged through, and the one they are in now, need to be considered. The phases of passive, active, and applied learning are a sound description of the quantity and quality of your kid's abilities.

Phase 1: Passive Learning—They have *seen it* done.

All good parents are aware of the importance of setting positive examples for their kids. We are their first models and most influential examples of what and how things are to be done.

We're all familiar with the phrase "Do as I say, not as I do," mainly in relation to our kids. Right? Actually, how often that is practiced is a revealing tell of a parent's behavior first, and then the child's. That's because kids of all ages are great imitators of their parents and possess an amazing appetite for passive learning through observation. Especially when the lessons are coming from the adults in the room.

Passive learning through observation is just what it sounds like. The process involves learning to do simple things by watching and listening to the way others do it—whatever "it" is. In the simplest of studies, kids don't even need to understand why something is being done or how it works. In their minds, if it works for their parents, it should work for them too.

One of our favorite personal stories about the power of observational learning happened when our son Reed was about four years old. Unbeknownst to us, he had decided to ditch his usual car-ride juice box beverage for a much stronger drink option. While pulling through our favorite drive-through coffee shop, Reed politely asked for his back seat car window to be rolled down. "Mom. Window down, please." After patiently waiting for the car to stop at the order window, Reed unexpectedly leaned forward as far as his buckles would allow and, without hesitation, placed his order from his seat. In a clear and sure voice, he called out his drink. "Um, yes, please. I'd like an iced grande mocha, no whip cream. Please." Shocked at the complexity and confidence of his order, both Mom and the barista burst into laughter. Still secured in his car seat, Reed smiled back at them and waited patiently for beans to grind and espresso shots to pull. A minute later, the still smiling barista delivered Reed a chocolate milk over ice. No coffee. Everyone was delighted.

It would be years before Reed would actually start drinking real coffee. But there was no denying he learned young how to order the stuff by watching and listening to the example set by his mom. From passively observing Mom order and savor her daily coffee, he came to believe the caffeinated drink is both an important and enjoyable start to every day.

Similarly, by passively watching us clean up around the house, he was first introduced to the "joys" of vacuuming. As soon as he was big enough to reach the handle, he wanted a turn at cleaning the floors, all the while insisting he could do it by himself. Likewise, hearing Mom and Dad speak kindly to one another modeled the value of using words like "please," "thank you," and "I love you." Reed's first introduction to coffee, cleaning, and kindness were all observational. Passive learning.

It's very important to let the power of our kids' passive-learning exposures sink deep into our often already made-up parent brains. Their wide eyes and open ears rarely miss a word we say or a thing we do. **What parents model by example becomes what our kids believe is acceptable.**

Have you seen the beloved holiday movie *A Christmas Story*? It's a tradition for many families to watch the film at least once in the final festive weeks of the year. Remember the part when young Ralphie is helping his father change a flat tire and he accidently lets "Oh, fudge!" slip from his lips? Only he didn't say fudge. Knowing he was in deep trouble, it comes as no surprise when in the following scene we find Ralphie sitting in the bathroom, bar of red Lifebuoy soap in his mouth, being questioned by his mom as to where in the world had he heard *that* word.

Before answering, Ralphie thought to himself, "Now I had heard that word at least ten times a day from my old man. My father worked in profanity the way other artists might work in oils or clay. It was his true medium. A master."[1]

As laughable and relatable Ralphie's slip of the tongue is to many adults, it also serves as a perfect reminder to us parents that our kids are quick to talk the talk and walk the walk that we model first. When our kids indeed follow our lead down the wrong path, it's important not to rest the full weight of blame square on their shoulders for what we showed them how to do. Or in Ralphie's

10 Things Kids Need to See and Hear
from Their Parents

Kids need to see their parents

1. Show appropriate physical affection with loved ones
2. Practice table manners
3. Vote
4. Read books
5. Unplug from digital devices
6. Share their time, talent, and treasures with those in need
7. Drive safely
8. Be patient in moments of frustration
9. Treat others as they want to be treated
10. Be present in the moment

Kids need to hear their parents

1. Say "I love you"
2. Congratulate others for their accomplishments
3. Laugh
4. Speak kindly to others
5. Speak kindly about others
6. Offer authentic apologies
7. Ask questions
8. Use a calm tone when others are loud
9. Say "I'm proud of you"
10. Pray

case, what his father did at least ten times a day, right in front of him.

As illustrated, parent modeling is powerful and should be the primary source of passive learning for our children. So obviously we should be providing them with a steady stream of positive examples to learn from. The quantity of information they save in the complex network of their rapidly changing brain is seemingly limitless. The saying "You can never have too much of a good thing" can be applied to a child's need to see their parents modeling how to do good. All kinds of good. When parents perform the skills used to confidently handle the many demands of life, kids feel they have permission to try doing the same for themselves. From completing household chores to showing kindness to strangers, making it to work on time to obeying traffic laws, kids are watching and learning from parents what they'll need to one day master for themselves.

One last thought about how passive learning works. The next time your untamed teen rolls their eyes and huffs in your general direction a saucy "I know!" pause and consider what they really mean. Coated in an abrasive layer of sass, what they might be unsuccessfully saying is that they believe their brain has been sufficiently briefed on the subject. And you know what, it's probably true.

Their brains may indeed *know* how proper chopping with a kitchen knife works or *why* it's *so important* to turn a corner without running the car's back tire up on the curb. The hours they sat in driver's ed class weren't a total waste of time. The yearlong pandemic quarantine they spent with you watching every single cooking show Netflix ever produced stuffed their brains with all the passive learning their heads could possibly handle. Yet, when the rubber meets the road/curb or the knife blade slices back, their limited experience begins to show. That's because they have yet to pair the passive-learning theory in their head with the active learning experience required to in fact perform the tasks. In Real Life.

Phase 2: Active Learning—They *can do* it.

The simple truth of the matter is, where passive learning builds knowledge, active learning is required to build skills. Much to the frustration of know-it-all kids of all ages, there is only one way to convert the long list of their passive learning "I know" statements into "I can" abilities. There are no shortcuts. Parents can't purchase their kid an easy-pass upgrade to speed things along, and no amount of bribery can get incapable kids moved up in the ranks of proficiency. To develop the kinds of skills needed to succeed in life, your child must commit themselves to physically engaging in their learning process. They'll need some real hands-on experience. Instruction and practice are the two key ingredients of active learning. Time behind the wheel learning from an experienced driver is the exact opposite of riding as a parent's passenger for fifteen or sixteen years. Getting into the kitchen to prep a meal with a seasoned cook is a completely different experience than waiting around for the call to dinner. The same goes for nearly all hands-on activities. Our best learning comes from quality instructions, personal interactions, experiments, role-playing, and constructive evaluations that include a second chance at performing the same task. Each additional performance further links the passive-learning knowledge stored in your child's head with higher levels of physical achievement and personal development.[2]

There are no known savants with eidetic imagery (popularly called a photographic memory) who can do with their hands what they recall in their head, without any previous practice. This makes the odds very high that your child will need to hone their studied skills through a series of interactive and often repeated trainings. As we tend to repeat what we remember and remember what we repeat, it's important to help your kids see active learning is more than just a one-and-done experience.

Just because they helped cook dinner once, last week, doesn't mean they know their way around the kitchen. Hanging a framed picture on the wall isn't the only carpentry skill they'll ever need. Checking boxes on a medical history form for school is just the tip of the iceberg compared to a visit to the doctor's office. Your kid saying, "I already did that," or "Not this again," offers insufficient evidence of their true abilities.

The simple fact of the matter is, skillsets are built by repeatedly engaging in active-learning lessons. Often.

While researching and writing two of our previous books for teens, *The Manual to Manhood* and *The Girls' Guide to Conquering Life*, we interviewed hundreds of world-class experts and professionals in many fields. One of the recurring messages the top chefs, stylists, builders, designers, financiers, doctors, entrepreneurs, and professional athletes shared with us was the importance of practice. Interestingly, not one repeated the saying "Practice makes perfect." Why? Because they all know that where the claim "practice makes perfect" is an unforgettably sticky statement, it also isn't true. Agreeably they all attribute their success to the fact that **practice makes *better* and a lot of practice made them the best.**

Take the example shared by one of auto racing's top pit crew team members. In less time than it takes to read this paragraph, a NASCAR pit crew can change four 58-pound tires on a race car. That's just a few seconds spent changing each wheel. How do they get so fast? Practice. But how does speed mechanics relate to the skills your child needs to become a more confident and capable driver? By focusing on the basics. Here's some great advice shared by the best tire changers in the world: *Have your kids practice changing a car's tire in the safety of your driveway so they don't have to learn while stranded on the side of the freeway.*

Phase 3: Applied Learning—They *can teach* it.

Use what you know. Do what you can. Solve the problem or make the most of the opportunity. Applied learning is the union of passive and active learning in an environment that increases your child's motivation and sparks their interest in sharing their skills with others in ways that provide solutions to real-world demands. To get the most out of applied learning, it's best that your child interacts with others. Making decisions as a group, in team events, and with crowd reinforcement are all important settings for demonstrating that they aren't just good on their own (independent), they are better when working together (interdependent).

Skillset Maturity Continuum

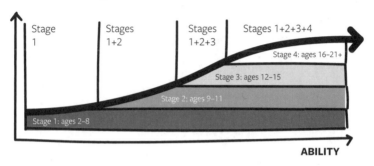

The next few chapters are dedicated to a long list of life skills that, when mastered, build kids' confidence and capabilities over time. With the day in mind that your child will step to the edge and take the big leap out of the nest, we call this catalog of basic abilities needed to soar the Launch List.

The abilities on the list are layered into four stages appropriate to kids' ages on the Skillset Maturity Continuum. Each individual ability is given a skill level rating of between 0 and 3. The lowest number of 0 indicates that your child is either too young or has no experience with that particular task. The rating of 1 means your child has seen the skill done (passive learning), while 2 indicates they can do it for themselves (active learning), and 3 implies they could teach the skill to someone else (applied learning).

In the next six chapters you'll see how the Launch List of over 300 combined skillsets and toolsets are intended to be introduced at different stages of development. You know your kid and their capabilities best. So please use the Launch List as a guide rather than a rule. It is *not* a rigid program. Instead, think of it as the process. By teaching your kid over time how to properly handle life's many demands, you are enabling them to grow and mature in age- and ability-appropriate stages. Whereas those short on time may find trying to cram everything in last minute may get a bit difficult.

In the end, the Launch List is only a beginning. Use it to give your kid a strong start at any stage. And remember, **their greatness tomorrow begins with your guidance today.**

Skill Level Ratings

0 = Not Yet (Too Young or No Experience)

1 = Seen It (Passive Learning)

2 = Can Do (Active Learning)

3 = Can Teach (Applied Learning)

Here are a few everyday examples of age-appropriate abilities and how well a child might perform a specific task.

A six-year-old child is right in the middle of Stage 1 on the Skillset Maturity Continuum.

- Once they have learned to ride a bike and can safely pedal around on their own, they would receive an ability rating of 2 = Can Do (Active Learning).

A ten-year-old kid is in Stage 2.

- By watching a parent change a baby's diaper but having no diaper changing experience themselves, this ten-year-old would receive an ability rating of 1 = Seen It (Passive Learning).

A thirteen-year-old is in Stage 3.

- If they have ever clogged a toilet, freaked out, and refused to fix the problem because they don't know how to use a plunger, they would receive an ability rating of 0 = Not Yet. On the other hand, if they kept their cool and cleared the blockage with a toilet plunger, you could give them a rating of 2 = Can Do (Active Learning).

A nineteen-year-old is in Stage 4.

- When they vote in an election and take their younger sibling to the polls with them to demonstrate the importance of democracy, they would receive an ability rating of 3 = Can Teach (Applied Learning).

7. THE LAUNCH LIST—STAGE 1

THE BASICS, AGES 2–8

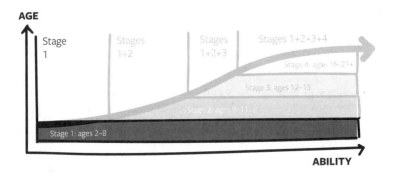

Between the Ages of 2 and 8 Years Old

As with any sound developmental process, it's best to begin with the basics. Guiding kids to value the importance of mastering the fundamentals is not an exercise reserved for sports coaches and music teachers. We parents are the first and most significant influencers in the development of our children's character and their learning the everyday life skills they will need to practice from time to time, over their lifetime.

Most parents have fond memories of their child looking up at them with delight in their eyes while proclaiming, "I did it all by myself!" Like the first time they tied their own shoes, fastened their own seat belt, or wiped up a juice spill. Then there are the times they fed the dog an afternoon snack equal to a week's worth of kibble, slathered every inch of their body with an expensive bottle of lotion, or called Grandma at 4:30 a.m. just to say hi. All by themselves. Well, despite what most of us over the age of a single digit remember about learning to do the easy things for the first time, getting from "I can't do" to "I can do" is not as simple as we may think. But it can be fun.

Parents and researchers agree, young children learn best through play. Actually, we all engage in learning more readily and deeply when we are having a good time. As kids play, they are naturally developing gross and fine motor skills, practicing creative problem solving, and learning how to engage and get along with other people.[1] Though not all of life's basic daily tasks can be made into a game, when parents invite kids into learning how to do things in a fun and interactive way, the lessons stick tighter and last longer. So whenever possible, **make the learning lessons less of a lecture and more of an interactive fun adventure.**

Without a doubt, kids can start "helping out" around the house as young as two years old. Much of what they can learn to do should be supervised and will seldom be done with great precision. Still, helping to pick up toys after a playdate or putting clean jammies away in a dresser drawer are easy to learn and translate well into future skills that some teens still struggle to complete.

The following is the Launch List of Stage 1 abilities. Everything is age appropriate for kids between 2 and 8 years old to start learning and start practicing. Notice we said start practicing. The abilities listed in Stage 1 can be taught young and then should be practiced for a lifetime. As can be expected when learning anything new, young children's skill level will most likely start with a low rating. Then as they learn and practice the Stage 1 abilities, you can increase their skill level from a Not Ready rating of 0 or 1 up to a Ready rating of 2 or 3.

THE LAUNCH LIST STAGE 1: Ages 2–8	Skill Level			
Abilities (ages 2–8)	Not Yet 0	Seen It 1	Can Do 2	Can Teach 3
1. Answer phone politely				
2. Assist with making the bed				
3. Assist with watering plants				
4. Bring in the mail				
5. Brush teeth				
6. Clean up light spills				
7. Comb hair				
8. Dial phone numbers				
9. Dial 911 in an emergency				
10. Dust surfaces				
11. Feed family pets				
12. Hang towel after bath or shower				
13. Help move clothes from washer to dryer				
14. Help separate and fold laundry				
15. Help with weeding a garden				
16. Know home street address				
17. Know own age and birthday				
18. Know parent's phone number				
19. Learn to swim				
20. Make a sandwich				
21. Participate in selecting day's clothes and getting dressed				
22. Pick up and put away toys				
23. Prepare a midday snack				
24. Put dirty clothes in hamper				
25. Read a clock (digital and analog)				
26. Replace toilet paper roll				
27. Ride a bike				
28. Say "yes, please," "thank you," and "no, thank you"				
29. Set and clear kitchen table				
30. Shake hands politely				
31. Take a shower				
32. Wash hands				
33. Write a simple thank-you note				
Additional abilities:				

When reviewing the abilities and ranking your child's skill levels, please don't view the Launch List as a reminder of what your kids aren't doing yet. Instead, see it as a way to celebrate all they are capable of and to set goals for what they will soon be accomplishing. Also keep in mind that the Launch List is not a complete catalog of everything your child will need to succeed in life. You will find that some abilities important to your family or your child's uniqueness may not be listed. Not a problem. You can add them yourself.

1. Answer phone politely

Ring. Ring.

"Hello." 👍

Ring. Ring.

"Yah, what." 👎

Practice makes better, so work with your kids on how to answer the phone politely. Do you want them to share their name? How much personal info should they give to a caller they don't know? What should they say when someone isn't available or not home? Is it okay for them to yell across the house that "some lady is calling about your car's extended warranty!"?

2. Assist with making the bed

Not everyone makes their bed every day. Some think, why bother when you'll just climb back in and mess it up tonight. Others prefer the clean and tidy look a made bed gives the room. Either way, making a bed is a good life skill to teach kids, because we all need to know at least one of the day's accomplishments will be there to welcome us back at the end of the day.

> **Helpful Hint:** A fun printed blanket or comforter cover that your young child really likes and wants to see each day can help inspire them to make their bed in the mornings. Think of what is displayed on their bed as part of their room's theme or personal style.

3. Assist with watering plants

Caring for plants is a simple way for kids to start learning about how living things grow. Whenever possible, have young kids help with caring for fast-growing plants like flowers and vegetables. This way they can see the fruits of their labor grow at a rate that is noticeable and tangible. Regularly watering plants will help your child develop patience, empathy, respect, and a sense of responsibility. A good safety rule when bringing any plant into a home or garden shared by a young child is to avoid anything even mildly poisonous.

4. Bring in the mail

The opposite of junk mail is fun mail. To encourage your child to help bring in the mail, make a trip to the mailbox memorable by regularly writing and sending them a stamped letter. Share something simple yet personal that they can post on the fridge or keep with their special things worth saving.

5. Brush teeth

Orange juice–flavored toothpaste. Now there's an idea that kids might really like. While few people enjoy breakfast with the flavor of *minty fresh* still lingering in their mouth, it may be the best thing to do for your child's overall oral health. While your child slept, plaque-causing bacteria multiplied by the millions in their sweet little mouth. The putrid proof can be smelled on the stench of their morning breath and seen clinging like pale moss to their once pearly whites. Brushing bacteria free before breakfast rids the mouth of overnight plaque and bacteria while coating tooth enamel with a protective barrier against sugary breakfast cereal and acidic juice. In the wise words of your family dentist, "Remember, kids, you only have to brush the teeth you want to keep."

> **Toothbrush Tech:** There are some very playful and affordable toothbrush designs for kids available at most stores these days. With flashing lights and fun songs playing as they brush, your child will enjoy a clean mouth more when it's also fun to hum along.

6. Clean up light spills

Kids are natural-born spillers. That's because their fine motor skills are far from adult-level coordination. So count on them spilling about anything and everything they get their hands on for more than a few years. Instead of running around behind them cleaning up like a hyper maid, try creating a child-sized station with child-sized supplies they can use to practice cleaning up after themselves. Show them how to use a sponge or cloth, and rather than scold them again for another spill, praise their efforts to wipe things up. That and when you discover them sitting on the kitchen floor in a pile of all-purpose flour, be sure to smile and get a few pictures before assisting them in the cleanup.

7. Comb hair

Different types of hair require different types of combs or brushes. Buying ones that work for your child's hair type will help their locks, curls, mop, or mane look and feel tangle-free as painlessly as possible. If hair care turns out to be a real time sucker and is often accompanied by alligator tears, seek help from the pros. Ask your barber or salon stylist for any tips or tricks they can share about caring for your child's hair.

8. Dial phone numbers

There's a big difference between dialing a landline phone and a cell phone. Teaching your kids to do both may take some creativity, but it will be well worth the effort. A fun way to show young children how to dial a phone is by sticking Post-it notes on a table or wall in the shape of a big keypad. Each Post-it gets an individual number. With a little practice, your kid will get dialing phone numbers down in no time. Once they do, you know what comes next? It's time to call the grandparents.

9. Dial 911 in an emergency

Calling for help from a police officer, a firefighter, or an EMT is a very serious event. Telling your child that 911 is a special phone number and is to be used only in an emergency is just the beginning. You also need to define what exactly is and isn't considered an emergency. They'll need to know how to dial a phone and what to say if they ever do need to make the call. It's a good plan to role-play and rehearse calling 911 on a toy or phone line that will not connect with an emergency operator. You take on the role of operator and instruct your child how to share important information and to do whatever the 911 operator tells them.

10. Dust surfaces

It's a common misconception that everyday household dust is made up of mostly shed human skin. In fact, it's not. Most dust in your home gets tracked in and drifts in from outdoors. Dirt, pollen, and soot all come from outside, while carpet fuzz, textile fibers, pet dander, and hair particles only make up about one-third of that dust layer atop your refrigerator. While dusting high spaces is best left for grown-ups, your kids are the perfect height to help clean lower-level surfaces like chair legs, side tables, and baseboards.

11. Feed family pets

The Centers for Disease Control and Prevention recommends kids younger than 5 years old should not touch pet food, treats, or grooming supplies. This is because children are at greater risk of contracting illness from contaminated feeding bowls and pet food due to the likelihood of them touching their mouths and face with dirty fingers while their immune systems are still developing.[2] When older kids do feed pets, they should always wash their hands with soap and water after.

Quick Tip: Work together to make a pet care chart. Creating a fun way to know if the pets got fed, who took who for a walk, and if it's time for a flea bath will help keep every member of the family happy and healthy.

12. Hang towel after bath or shower

Kids' bath and shower towels should be hung to dry after each use and washed after only three to five normal uses. Allowing dirty towels to air-dry before throwing them in the hamper will help prevent unwelcome and often smelly growth of bacteria and fungi.[3] To help your child remember to refresh their towel regularly, create an easy-to-follow chores chart and add Change Bath Towels to specific days of the week.

13. Help move clothes from washer to dryer

Average American families do between eight and ten loads of laundry per week. Each load takes about an hour and thirty minutes to wash and dry. That means most homes spend over fifteen hours a week washing, rinsing, drying, and repeating. That's upwards of thirty-two and a half days doing laundry a year. That's more than a month! Makes you really appreciate that washer and dryer.

14. Help separate and fold laundry

To most families, folding clothes fresh from the dryer feels like a never-ending contest. The good news for semi-pro and new-to-the-game rookie folders alike is that as soon as kids know the difference between shirts and pants—yours and theirs—they can join in the "game."

> **Helpful Hint:** Teach your kids early that reading the garment tag for care instructions is important. When in doubt, hang-drying their favorite shirt beats accidently shrinking it down to an unwearable size.

15. Help with weeding a garden

A fun fact about weeds that will amaze your kids: The largest weed in the world is the giant hogweed. Found mainly in Central Asia, hogweeds can reach up to twelve feet high and grow leaves thirty-six inches long. Now that's a big weed.

16. Know home street address

Each child develops differently, so there isn't a hard-and-fast rule for when your kid will be able to recall their family's home address. Yet if you start practicing young, by the time they are between four and six years old, they should have your home's street address fully memorized.

> **Helpful Hint:** One fun memory trick to learning and remembering a street address is to turn it into a rhythm or rhyme. Kids love to clap and sing along, so don't hesitate to tap, rap, or turn your home address into a sticky little jingle they just can't get out of their head.

17. Know own age and birthday

Why can't kids remember the birthday gift you gave them last year? Because they are too focused on the present. ☺ But seriously, kids love knowing how old they are and when they will celebrate aging up a year. Make learning their age and birthday sticky by talking about how important the day they were born is to you. How on [*insert date*] they were born [*insert number of years*] ago, and how on that day they made you the happiest person in the whole wide world!

18. Know parent's phone number

The power of your child's memory is boosted when information is put to a catchy tune. Singing your phone number to your kids can help them lock it away and recall it again easily.

19. Learn to swim

Not only is swimming good fun and great exercise, the act can save a kid's life. According to the National Safe Kids Campaign, childhood drowning is the second leading cause of unintentional injury-related death in kids up to the age of fourteen years old.[4] A skill that can be enjoyed for a lifetime, formal swim lessons are recommended for children when they are about four years old, while water-safety lessons should be taught to children of all ages.

20. Make a sandwich

Peanut butter and jelly. Meat and cheese. Crust on or crust off. Whole or cut in half. The number of ways your child can enjoy a sandwich is about as endless as their imagination. Sure they may need a step stool to reach the counter or some help putting the mustard back in the fridge, but that's a fair trade for them learning how to build the sandwich of their dreams for lunch or an after-school snack.

21. Participate in selecting day's clothes and getting dressed

Some kids go for a new look every day while others are perfectly happy wearing the same thing again. Either way, giving your child a voice in deciding what they will wear is an important part of them developing confidence in their personal identity. To help them dress well, avoid making outfit decisions when time is short. Instead, pick a time of day when outfit options can be made calmly and creatively. Laying clothes out the night before can be fun and helps reduce getting-dressed stress on busy mornings.

22. Pick up and put away toys

The toughest people on the planet are LEGO walkers. Not an official sport or recognized profession, LEGO walkers are the society of pain-stricken parents who have stepped barefoot, full weight down, on the colorful plastic pieces left behind following some very creative play. To avoid an unwilling initiation into the club, teach your child to pick up their toys while you are both still young. Here are a few less-painful-than-LEGO-walking ways to encourage your kids to pick up and put away their toys.

- ☐ **Give toys specific places to be put away.** It's important your child knows what needs to be picked up and where it goes. Giving the process of picking up toys some order will keep your child from guessing if they did it right or not.
- ☐ **Starting young, show kids how it's done.** As soon as your child can walk and grasp, they can help clean up. Show them how, with a little modeling by getting down with them and setting a good example.
- ☐ **Make cleaning up fun.** Kids like to play. That's how all those toys got spread out all over the place. Make a game out of picking up and be sure to smile and laugh as much as possible.

☐ **Stay positive.** Instead of saying, "There will be no snack until you get all these toys put away!" try something more like, "After your toys are picked up, we can pick out a snack together."

23. Prepare a midday snack

"I'm hungry."

"What's there to eat around here?"

"There's never anything I like to eat in this house!"

Get used to hearing all of the above as your kid stands in front of an open fridge or cupboard doors. What they are really asking is, can they have a snack. To help them get used to making a midday snack for themselves, include them in the grocery shopping and snack prep. Having them help you pick out and prepare their snacks will give them some control over managing their between-meals munchies in a healthy and portion-appropriate way.

24. Put dirty clothes in hamper

Depending on how active, sweaty, and prone to stains your child is, their dirty clothes hamper can fill up quick. Giving kids their own hamper can help keep their dirty clothes off the floor and give them a tangible way to see when it's time to do laundry. So what should they put in the hamper and when?

☐ **Pajamas** should hit the hamper after three or four nights.

☐ **Underwear and socks** get only one-day wear.

☐ **T-shirts, tank tops, and camisoles** should be washed after each wearing.

☐ **Jeans** can usually make it three wears before washing.

☐ **Leggings and tights** should be washed after wearing to help keep them fresh and relieve baggy knees.

☐ **Bathing suits** should be washed after that day's dip.

☐ **Bedsheets** should be washed weekly, or more often if your child sleeps hot and sweats a lot.

25. Read a clock (digital and analog)

To help your child learn to tell time, start by practicing counting to 60, one number at a time. Next, move to counting up to 60 by 5, 10, 15, and 30 to help them learn how we break time up within an hour. Don't worry if they don't get the concept of the big and little hand or why there's a ":" between the numbers on the clock. With some practice and *time*, they'll get it.

Just Joking

Q: What did the second hand say to the hour hand as it passed by?

A: See you in a minute.

26. Replace toilet paper roll

Second only to the debate about the toilet paper hanging over (in front of) or under (behind) is the dispute of who's responsible for replacing an empty roll. Depending on the type of toilet paper holder in the bathroom, your kids really should be up for the task of swapping out a cardboard tube for a fresh round of wipes. Some spring-loaded roll holders can be difficult for little fingers to manage while the slide-on-and-off dispensers are easy picking for kids of all ages. What absolutely doesn't work is a bare tube, not a square to spare, when "business" is concluded.

Quick tips to wipe out toilet paper issues in your home:

1. Keep extra rolls close. Some toilet paper stands double as a roll caddy.
2. Incentivize the swap. Offer a TP Treat to the child who replaces the roll without being asked.
3. Make a trade. Each time the cardboard is left hanging, swap a new roll for some extra duties that need to get done around the house.

27. Ride a bike

There is no right age to learn how to ride a bike. Some children as young as four years old have the balance, dexterity, leg strength, and understanding of basic instructions to give a two-wheeler a go. Other kids discover around their sixth birthday that they are physically and emotionally prepared to take the training wheels off. When exactly your child starts to pedal on their own doesn't really matter. The good news is, once they learn to ride a bike, they'll never forget. That's because recalling how to ride comes from experiences stored in our procedural memory banks. As the name implies, procedural memories are responsible for performance. Typically preserved for a lifetime, the procedural memories your child forms each time they ride a bike are hardly ever compromised, meaning they're not easily forgotten. Wouldn't it be great if the same were true about their memory of the bike lock combination?

28. Say "yes, please," "thank you," and "no, thank you"

Good manners matter. A well-timed please or thank you won't cost your child a thing. Yet knowing and using their manners can help them make great gains in life. The best way to teach your child good manners is to model the behavior you want to see them practice. By making manners a normal part of life, you won't need to be concerned if they know when and whom to use them around.

29. Set and clear kitchen table

A family that eats together, bonds together. Research into nutrition has found that "eating with others, particularly family, is associated with healthier dietary outcomes" in both children and adults[5] and that sharing meals together is essential to family bonding and the development of ethical children.[6]

30. Shake hands politely

A confident handshake is an important part of practicing good manners and making a good first impression. When kids know how to shake hands, adults are usually impressed. Practice shaking hands with your child by

117

teaching them the difference between a good and bad handshake. No dead fish, Hulk grips, or dainty fingers. Just a sound hand-to-hand greeting with as much eye contact as they can manage.

31. Take a shower

At a certain age, your kid may feel too old for a parent-led scrub-a-dub, yet you know they're still too young to bathe themselves unsupervised. For many parents, the logical next best way to get their kids clean, while giving them the independence and privacy they want, is to teach them how to take a shower. A proper shower. A "get everything wet, wash their hair with shampoo, scrub the dirt and stink off with soap" kind of shower. Without good instructions, many parents find their kids are just as dirty when they step out of the shower as they were when they turned the water on.

How are you not wet?

Did you even touch the soap?

What did you do in there for twenty minutes?

Teaching your child how to wash in a shower, from head to toe and under their arms, will not only help them look and smell better, it can keep your water and energy bill from draining your budget.

> **Quick Tip:** Setting a timer for five to fifteen minutes can help your child begin to understand and manage their play vs. wash time in the shower.

32. Wash hands

All parents know, what's on a kid's hands will eventually make it into their mouth. That's reason enough to make frequent handwashing a regular part of your child's life, starting young. Get your kids in the healthy habit of washing their hands for twenty seconds with soap and water . . .

☐ *after* playing with a pet, using the bathroom, sneezing, coughing, or blowing their nose;

☐ *before* and *after* preparing food;

☐ *before* eating or touching everything that is headed into their mouth.

> **Helpful Hint:** One way to make 20 seconds of handwashing fly by for young kids is to sing a round of the "Baby Shark" song, or modify the lyrics of "If You're Happy and You Know It" to include "wash your hands."

33. Write a simple thank-you note

Just a few kind words can go such a long way—literally if the thank-you note your child writes is mailed to out-of-town grandparents. A simple thank-you note is a great way to show someone they are appreciated. For kids who are too young to write, have them draw a picture instead. You know scribbling out "thx" or "luv U" to family or friends guarantees that note will hang on the refrigerator for at least a year. Most important, you are teaching your child to share their appreciation for others in a way that feels like a handcrafted hug.

Just Joking

You know you're an exhausted parent when "washing" yourself with wet wipes and calling it a "shower" feels perfectly acceptable.

A toddler can do more in an unsupervised minute than most people can do all day.

Ninety percent of parenting is wondering when you'll be able to lay down for more than five minutes again.

A two-year-old child is kind of like a running blender, without the top.

When your first child is born you become a parent. When your second child is born you become a referee.

8. THE LAUNCH LIST—STAGE 2
ELEMENTARY, AGES 9–11

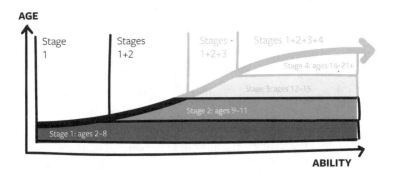

Between the Ages of 9 and 11 Years Old

Too big to be little yet still too little to be big, switching from a single- to double-digit birthday can be an odd time for kids and parents alike. Just a few years ago they were asking to be carried, and in a few years from now they'll be begging to drive. Their growing desire for independence from family and increased interest in friends is a sure sign that some big changes for everyone in your home are just around the corner. Soon they will be telling you they want a new cell phone and you'll be saying you're not ready for them to start puberty. Their bodies are getting stronger and so is the peer pressure about deciding who's in and who's out of their friend groups. Academics, sports, music, and clubs all take on deeper meaning and require more time of everyone in the family. Strangest of all, "liking" someone starts to take on entirely new meaning. Yep, all this and more is happening.

What came naturally when they were younger now requires some extra effort. Purposefully spending time together in environments where you can talk about friends, aspirations, accomplishments, and their concerns is essential to staying connected relationally. So is just having fun, no deep conversation strings attached.

Meet your kid's friends and their families. Car rides, invitations to events, and overnights at a friend's homes can all be part of this age, so be sure you trust the people they are with when you are not around. Teaching them good manners, respect, a sense of right and wrong, and what behaviors both you and they know are acceptable will make the time they spend with friends and their families worth repeating.

Finally, **praise your child in public and discipline them in private.** Something we all share in common is the desire to gain respect and avoid embarrassment. If they are not yet concerned about what others think of them, they likely soon will be. Everyone occasionally says or does the wrong thing in front of others. Public shaming can be deeply hurtful. So, when your child makes a mistake that needs addressing, take them aside to correct their behavior in a way that allows them to feel safe, right their wrong, learn from the mistake, and see you are there to help them discover and become their very best.

THE LAUNCH LIST STAGE 2: Ages 9–11	Skill Level			
Abilities (ages 9–11)	Not Yet 0	Seen It 1	Can Do 2	Can Teach 3
All abilities in previous stage				
34. Address an envelope and mail with postage				
35. Assist with meal preparations				
36. Change a baby's diaper				
37. Change a light bulb				

Abilities (ages 9–11)	Not Yet 0	Seen It 1	Can Do 2	Can Teach 3
38. Change bed sheets				
39. Clean bathroom sink, tub, and toilet				
40. Clean glass and mirrors				
41. Clean kitchen table, counters, and sink				
42. Clean up after pet				
43. Do yardwork with hand tools				
44. Empty trash and recycling				
45. Fold and hang clean clothing				
46. Get up with an alarm				
47. Give confident handshake with eye contact				
48. Introduce themselves casually				
49. Leave a voicemail				
50. Load and empty dishwasher				
51. Make and count change				
52. Make bed				
53. Make breakfast				
54. Make lunch				
55. Manage personal hygiene				
56. Order from a menu				
57. Pack a sack lunch				
58. Plant garden and houseplants				
59. Practice goal setting and progress tracking				
60. Put groceries away				
61. Select day's clothes without assistance				
62. Separate the laundry				
63. Set a clock				
64. Sweep and dust-mop hard floors				
65. Use kitchen appliances				
66. Use kitchen knife				
67. Vacuum carpeted floors				
68. Walk pet				
69. Water plants, indoors and out				
70. Wet-mop floors				
71. Write a formal thank-you note				
Additional abilities:				

34. Address an envelope and mail with postage

In today's world of direct messaging, email, and communicating with emojis, knowing how to legibly print an address on an envelope and sticking sufficient postage in the corner may seem like a thing of the past. That is, until the know-how is needed to send thank-you notes, packages, or original documents from here to there in three-to-five business days. In the end, the key to teaching kids to successfully mail anything hinges on their handwriting. Can the post office even read their writing? If so, they will be good to go. If not, their parcel could get sent to a special postal branch that deciphers illegible addresses. One at a time. No joke. Over five million pieces of mail per day.

35. Assist with meal preparations

Food is so much more than fuel. In our ever-busy, simple-seeking ways, some people have forgotten that mealtime should also be family time. Breakfast, lunch, and dinner are about so much more than just feeding the body. Preparing and enjoying meals together is also an excellent way to nourish the family's mind, heart, and soul. One fun way to draw your kids into the kitchen is to have them help create meal-themed music playlists. Listening to Caliente Cantiña on Taco Tuesdays and Italian Café on pizza night will make the kitchen the hottest spot in the house.

Here are a few kitchen rules that will help your kids become far more than good cooks.

Kitchen Rules

THERE ARE NO SECRET FAMILY RECIPES.
The chef is always right. Usually.
All flavors are good flavors.
Laughter is the most important ingredient.
THE ANSWER TO "CAN I TASTE IT?" IS ALWAYS YES.
Those who cook the meal get to name the meal.
THOSE WHO COMPLAIN ABOUT THE MEAL
GET TO COOK THE NEXT ONE.
There's always room at the table for one more.
Plate every dish with an extra serving of love.
Manners matter.

36. Change a baby's diaper

Surprise!

Seriously?

That's so gross!

All perfectly normal, perfectly healthy, first time and every time thereafter responses to changing a baby's dirty diaper. No matter how old you are. So, teaching your kid the proper use of wet wipes, powder, and stay-snug fastening is really all about welcoming them into the rotation of taking care of business on the business end of their little brother or sister.

37. Change a light bulb

Q. How many kids does it take to change a light bulb?

A. That depends on watt-age they are.

Well, watt-ever the age of your kid, if they are old enough to be trusted around electricity, it's time they learn how to change a light bulb. Of course, this is a task best taught and practiced a few times under the careful supervision of a responsible adult who knows the righty tighty, lefty loosey standard of an Edison screw. A bright rule to follow is when unscrewing a bulb, grasp it like an egg. Just enough to hold on, yet not so tight that it cracks or brakes.

38. Change bed sheets

How often should kids' bed sheets be changed? Good question. Past the nighttime "accident" phase, most parents agree with the experts' recommendation of a weekly changing of the sheets. It doesn't take long for your kid's bed to collect a truly grody amount of dirt, hair, pet fur, food crumbs, dander, sweat, and drool between the sheets. But most parents admit to waiting as long as twenty-five days before swapping in a fresh set. Changing the bed once a week helps cut down on the amount of germs and allergens your kids are exposed to all night long.

39. Clean bathroom sink, tub, and toilet

One sure way to inspire your kid to put the cap back on the toothpaste, aim into the toilet, and pull the shower curtain closed all the way is to have them take over cleaning the bathroom once a week. Putting on sanitary gloves and squirting nontoxic spray cleaners may not be considered fun but neither is using a messy bathroom. Add *Clean Bathroom* to the chores chart and work together for a week or two to get them trained.

40. Clean glass and mirrors

Kid-safe cleaners are available most everywhere these days. Show your kids how a little "wax-on, wax-off" cleaning is an effective way to wipe spots and fingerprints from both glass and mirrors. They can do the lower half and you'll handle the top half.

41. Clean kitchen table, counters, and sink

Messing up the kitchen can be fun. Cleaning up afterward, not so much. Unless you make it manageable and measurable. Try breaking the kitchen into zones and having each cleaner, kids included, take on their area like a pro. To figure out who cleans what, play a game of spin the ketchup bottle. Wherever the top stops, that's your space to clean.

42. Clean up after pet

"Can we keep it? Please, please, please? I'll feed it every day and clean up any messes. Seriously. I promise." Well, it's time to hold your kids to their commitments. Pet messes are the nasty part of living with an animal. Dog, cat, lizard, hamster, and fish—they all require some cleaning up after from time to time.

It can't be any worse than changing a baby's diaper. Or can it?

43. Do yardwork with hand tools

The shovel and rake are willing and able to get the job done. All that is needed now is your kid's muscle power to help transplant that shrub. Teaching your kid how to properly use light hand tools while working in the yard is a great way to add curb appeal to your place while doing something good for the environment. There's nothing like a little dirt work to help them feel more connected to the earth. Dig in, kid.

44. Empty trash and recycling

Kids for sure know how to manage clearing the trash on their digital devices. How about from the house to the correct bins outside? If they can do it virtually, they can do it physically too. Making emptying the actual trash and recycling a daily get-done on the to-do list will help keep the kitchen, bathroom, and your kid's room looking and smelling fresh.

45. Fold and hang clean clothing

The laundry basket is for dirty clothes headed to the wash. It's not a grab basket of clean outfits. Key to folding and hanging clothes is to have available space for them to go, other than the floor. Dressers, shelves, and closets with extra hangers are the obvious answers but not always the easiest to access. So keep these spaces open and available by clearing out what no longer fits.

46. Get up with an alarm

In this age range, bedtimes are gradually getting later and later. School-work, sports, and social and family activities are chewing up more hours in the day than a good night's sleep seems to allow. This makes the average amount of sleep kids get to be about nine hours. To help their growing bodies and active minds get the most of what sleep they can get, here are a few things sleep experts suggest.

- ☐ Eliminate screen time starting one hour before bed (much harder said than done for many families).
- ☐ Follow a regular nighttime routine.
- ☐ Keep a regular sleep schedule for lights out and the wake-up alarm each day.

47. Give confident handshake with eye contact

There's nothing new about the palm-pressing tradition of shaking hands. From a polite introduction to warm congratulations, the handshake is best delivered with confidence and eye contact. For some kids, eye contact feels awkward. Show them that they don't have to stare the other person down or try to read their soul. Instead, a short second of eye contact confirms that they are interested in meeting, greeting, or complimenting another person.

48. Introduce themselves casually

Of all our daily blunders, few are more common than failing to make a simple social introduction. Offering a casual greeting that includes their name and a smile will help your kid comfortably break the ice and make a good first impression.

49. Leave a voicemail

As archaic as it may sound to kids today, some people actually do expect them to leave a message after the beep. Teachers, coaches, parents, and future bosses will want to know a few details about why they called. So teach your kid the three rules of leaving a voicemail in thirty seconds or less.

1. START WITH YOUR NAME.
2. BRIEFLY EXPLAIN THE REASON FOR YOUR CALL.
3. CLEARLY GIVE A CALLBACK NUMBER.

50. Load and empty dishwasher

One of the most contentious tasks in any kitchen is loading and unloading the dishwasher. Other than disagreements about whose turn it is, the leading reason we argue over the appliance has to do with *how* it's loaded. According to dishwasher manufacturers, the way people load a dishwasher is a reflection of their personality. Protectors make sure everything is in the proper place. Organizers load the racks like a game of Tetris. And curators go to great lengths to arrange the same plates, glasses, and silverware in order next to each other. Other than the basics of not blocking the sprayers, remembering the detergent, and pressing Start, there's really not much to the task. So don't let a clash of personalities get in the way of getting the dishes done. Instead, establish an easy-to-remember schedule of who and when the machine gets loaded and unloaded.

51. Make and count change

Who actually uses paper and coin money anymore? Not many. Still, learning how to count change has less to do with cash in hand and more to do with the concepts of basic math and simple problem-solving skills. Learning to make change can save your child the embarrassment of exchanging incorrect funds at a neighborhood garage sale, friend's lemonade stand, or cash-only food truck.

52. Make bed

When your kid makes their bed on their own in the morning, they are starting each day with a win. Their young brain thrives on accomplishments and the sense of pride that comes with success. To encourage them to get in the habit of conquering their first task of the day, make it personal. The print, pattern, or color of their blanket, comforter, and pillowcase can be a reflection of their unique personality and sense of style.

53. Make breakfast

It's the first meal of the day and you're not always available to make it for them. A bowl of cereal, scrambled egg, or fruit smoothie are all perfectly acceptable options, and your kid should know how to make them all. How else can you ever expect to get breakfast in bed on your next special day!

54. Make lunch

A sandwich, bowl of soup, or microwave burrito. There's always the leftover pizza from yesterday's movie night. Making lunch for themselves is a must-know for any kid whose stomach can't make it past noon without a refill. Get your child into the kitchen to help with lunch, then to make lunch on their own, and finally to prepare the midday meal for the rest of the family. Teach them the lunch-making basics and maybe, just maybe, you'll stop hearing them shout across the house, "What's for lunch?"

55. Manage personal hygiene

From the top of their head to the tip of their toes, your kid learning to manage their look, smell, and health is an important part of growing up.

Taking them shopping for soap, shampoo, toothpaste, combs, brushes, clippers, and trimmers that work best for them is just the first step. Next, help them get organized in how and where they keep their personal products in drawers, in cabinets, and on countertops. Remember, these are *personal* items. Sharing is not always caring when your kid has different self-care product preferences than you or their siblings.

56. Order from a menu

Any kid can point to the #4 meal deal on a wall-mounted catalog of fast food. Mature kids also know how to order from a menu without pictures. Learning to read through the course options, selecting a dish, and politely placing the order with the table's server may take some getting used to, but it will be well worth the effort. They'll like the freedom of ordering for themselves, and you'll enjoy knowing you can take them anywhere to eat.

57. Pack a sack lunch

A sandwich, fruit slices, carrots, maybe a small bag of chips. Sound familiar? If so, that's because many parents pack bites like this in their kid's school lunch almost every day. The repeating task of packing a midday meal is absolutely something your kid can be doing for themselves. Get them into the routine of preparing their next day's sack lunch the night before. This will help keep the inevitable morning rush from tipping into chaos.

58. Plant garden and houseplants

Repotting a houseplant. Seeding a garden. Watering and pruning. A little dirt under their fingernails will do your kid good. Teaching them the difference between potting and garden soil, sun versus shade plants, and the right time to pick a vegetable or prune a flower reinforces practicing patience, care, and consideration for something that takes time to grow.

59. Practice goal setting and progress tracking

Goals are much different than wishes. Your kid wishing they could get another pet or buy the latest and greatest fad thing with their own money is something that may or may not come true. Good thing your kids don't need to know magic to turn their wishful thinking into a tangible goal. They just need to make their goal specific, trackable, accountable, and worth celebrating when it is reached. For instance, setting a goal to save $50 in the next fifty days is a specific goal most kids can set, track, and complete. In order for your child to turn their goal into reality, they will need four things key to their financial success:

GOAL: Save $50 in the Next Fifty Days

☐ A way to earn at least $1.00 a day.

☐ A measuring system to account for the total dollars earned and number of days remaining.

☐ A safe place to keep their growing savings.

☐ A person who regularly meets with them to check on their progress, celebrate accomplishments, assist with problem solving, and encourage them along the way to achieving their goal. Having an accountability partner raises the likelihood that your child will achieve their goals to as high as 95 percent. That's almost a sure thing.

60. Put groceries away

Another trip to the grocery store. Another kitchen counter lined with bags of food. Nobody in sight to help unpack. Before your kids disappear from sight, set the expectation that everyone helps carry in the bags, chips in to restock the pantry, and loads the refrigerator. Maybe sweeten the deal by offering a tasty treat to all those who help until every last stick of butter, loaf of bread, and jug of juice is put away.

61. Select day's clothes without assistance

The clothes we wear can be an outward expression of our innermost thoughts and feelings. Some days you will be pleasantly surprised by the choice of your child's outfit. Other mornings you might be taken aback a bit or struck with a case of the giggles at what they are wearing. Rather than laughing out loud or sending them back to their room to change into something you like better, remember what they selected may be an expression of how they see themselves or the mood they are in that day. If absolutely necessary, try suggesting another easy mix-and-match option.

62. Separate the laundry
Darks. Lights. Hot. Cold. It doesn't take much time to separate the laundry. Nor does it to shrink your favorite sweater. Learning not to toss a white dress shirt in with a load of blue jeans is one lesson every kid should learn before they end up in the same spin cycle. The shirt and jeans, that is.

63. Set a clock
Setting a clock only takes a few seconds and is something that needs to be done a couple times a year, depending on where you live. Next time clocks need to spring forward or fall back an hour have your kids set the clocks in your house, car, and the little one on your wrist.

Just Joking

If a stopped clock is still right twice a day, does that mean the other 1,438 minutes are a waste of time?

64. Sweep and dust-mop hard floors
Most kids like odd animals. Maybe that's the reason why hedgehogs, pygmy goats, potbelly pigs, and even skunks have become acceptable, albeit unusual, family pets. One furry friend that remains unwelcome in most homes are those little dust bunnies that madly multiply under the couch and in the corners. Just as kids are perfectly capable of caring for all types of creatures, they are equally able to sweep and dust-mop hard floors to help keep things tame around the house.

65. Use kitchen appliances
The blender, toaster, and microwave. If your kid can master about any type of high tech out there, they can handle learning how to operate some of your kitchen's most basic appliances. Have them graduate from supervised

to self-sufficient as they demonstrate they can safely use, clean, and put away the kitchen appliances.

66. Use kitchen knife

Most homes' kitchen knives aren't that sharp. That's because most blades don't get their needed two to three sharpenings per year. Still, your kid needs to know how to handle a kitchen chef's knife properly if they are to ever help you slice and dice during meal prep. Paying attention and at least a little hand-eye coordination are key to them not needing a Band-Aid after attempting to cut apple slices for their school lunch. Teach them early that a knife is a tool to be used in the kitchen and never a toy to be played with.

67. Vacuum carpeted floors

"This chore sucks." If you haven't heard it already, your kid will say those exact words soon enough. At least you know they'll be thinking it every time it's their turn to vacuum the carpet. A good plan is to start them off with vacuuming their room once a week. Once they have the basic control down, they can move on to other carpeted parts of the house. Dirt, pet fur, glitter, string, hair, and almost anything imaginable will end up inside the dirt canister. So teach them how to clear the machine after every use.

68. Walk pet

Caring for a pet can be a big job for a kid. The kind, size, and behavior of the pet can make a big difference in the way a child interacts with them. Caring for a pet that needs daily walking is a great way to teach your child responsibility and to be empathetic to the needs of others.

69. Water plants, indoors and out

Caring for plants doesn't just help them look good, it helps us feel good too. Research on the benefits associated with caring for houseplants includes these:

- Interior plants contribute to healthier air indoors, which improves our physical well-being and comfort.
- Both indoor and outdoor plants make our surroundings look and feel more pleasant.

☐ Plant care has been associated with reduced stress, increased pain tolerance, and improved productivity in people.

70. Wet-mop floors

Every now and then, the kitchen, bathroom, or tile floors need a good cleaning. A little water, detergent, mop, and elbow grease can sure make a difference when your kid has the know-how. You don't have to teach them to swab the deck, but they should be able to handle mopping up a spilled soda before it leaves a sticky mess on the kitchen floor.

71. Write a formal thank-you note

Different from a casual note dropped in the mail to thank the grandparents for a birthday gift card, a formal thank-you note is, well, far more formal. Taking the time to teach your kid to carefully print and thoughtfully tailor their note to fit the circumstances will serve them well for a lifetime. Now is also a good opportunity to help them craft their signature.

Just Joking

Can't find your kids? Just take a seat on the toilet and they'll find you.

Before I had kids, I didn't know I could ruin someone's day by saying, "Get dressed, please."

Child: I'm scared. Can I please sleep with you?
Parent: No. I can't risk the monster following you into my room and eating us both.

I always knew I'd be a patient parent. Until I watched my child zip their own jacket.

"So, I only stepped away for like two seconds . . ."—the beginning of every parenting horror story involving kids, flour, and a dog in the kitchen.

9. THE LAUNCH LIST—STAGE 3

MIDDLE, AGES 12–15

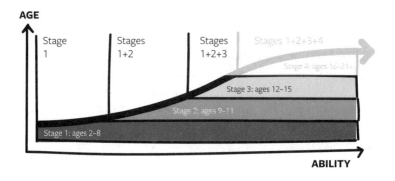

Between the Ages of 12 and 15 Years Old

From tween to teen in the blink of an eye. Remember when we were their age? Didn't life seem so much easier back then? Going to the mall, riding bikes, hanging out with friends, heading home for dinner when the streetlights came on. Oh, the good old days. All young teens today seem to be interested in is their phone, social media posts, and influencing meaningful change in the complex intersectionality of multiple overlapping factors of advantages and disadvantages in social identities that persist in the world today.

135

Come again?

Confused? Most parents of newly minted teens feel the same. One minute our kids are practicing the latest dance meme challenge and the next telling us about the ill effects of microplastics in the environment and their impact on marine life.

With greater access to a world of information than any generation prior, young teens today are drenched in an odd wash of childlike and adult-themed realities. From the hormone crushes of puberty to politically charged debates about immigration, their interests can sure cover a lot of ground for someone who's not yet able to drive.

As early teens navigate demanding changes physically, socially, and emotionally, they can benefit greatly from some purposeful, positive parenting. Kind, honest, open conversations about drinking, drugs, and sex may feel awkward at this age but, done right, can be very beneficial to both teens and parents. Respect is key. **When your teen feels their thoughts, feelings, and space are respected, they are more likely to extend the same to others.** Still, try to remember that there is no magic formula to guarantee easy days with your teenager. Yet there are a few beliefs that, when practiced by you as a parent, can help make the most of whatever comes their way—and yours:

- I believe you are your own person with unique interests, beliefs, and identities.
- I believe that what I say and the tone of voice I say it in matters. I choose kindness.
- There is nothing you can do that will make me love you any less.

THE LAUNCH LIST STAGE 3: Ages 12–15	Skill Level			
Abilities (ages 12–15)	Not Yet 0	Seen It 1	Can Do 2	Can Teach 3
All abilities in previous stages				
72. Apply deodorant or antiperspirant				
73. Brew coffee				
74. Brew tea				
75. Calculate a budget				
76. Calculate gratuity/tip				
77. Care for their feet				
78. Clean inside of car				
79. Clear a clogged sink or tub drain				
80. Clear a clogged toilet				
81. Cook dinner for themselves				
82. Cook meals for others				
83. Cook on outdoor grill				
84. Do yardwork with power tools				
85. Drive a nail with a hammer				
86. Fix a small hole in the wall				
87. Grocery shop with list				
88. Hang a picture				
89. Introduce other people casually				
90. Introduce other people formally				
91. Introduce themselves formally				
92. Iron clothes				
93. Learn CPR and basic first aid				
94. Locate a stud in the wall				
95. Make a bank deposit				
96. Manage a bank debit card account				
97. Manually open garage door from inside				
98. Memorize Social Security number				
99. Open bank account				
100. Open the door for another person				
101. Operate power hand tools				
102. Pack travel luggage for themselves				
103. Practice time management				
104. Pump gas				
105. Purchase a book of stamps				

Abilities (ages 12–15)	Not Yet 0	Seen It 1	Can Do 2	Can Teach 3
106. Read a level				
107. Read a tape measure				
108. Replace printer ink cartridge				
109. Sew on button				
110. Shave				
111. Spot-treat a stain				
112. Supervise younger siblings				
113. Take trash and recycling bins to curb for scheduled pickup				
114. Talk with a person with different beliefs				
115. Trim fingernails and toenails				
116. Turn off sink water lines				
117. Turn off toilet water line				
118. Type on a keyboard				
119. Use an adjustable wrench				
120. Wash a car				
121. Wash and dry cloths independently				
122. Wash dishes by hand				
123. Wrap a gift				
124. Write a formal invitation				
Additional abilities:				

72. Apply deodorant or antiperspirant

Helping your kids understand the difference between deodorant and antiperspirant should be easy. No sweat. Basically, deodorant acts as little more than an armpit air freshener and antiperspirant works like a sweat cork. Deodorants are classified as a cosmetic by the US Food and Drug Administration and are formulated to mask body odor. Antiperspirants work by introducing aluminum ions into the skin that interact with your kid's perspiration to squeeze sweat ducts closed. Your kid's best bet for beating their sweaty pit smell and wet stains is to stay clean, eat healthy, drink plenty of water, and try different types of underarm applications till they find the one that works for them.

73. Brew coffee

Knowing how to transform hot water and ground beans into "energy," comfort, and normalcy is a blessing to anyone who enjoys coffee. Though your kid may still be a bit young to drink the dark stuff, knowing how to brew a pot or pull a shot can be a good way to help get things going for older family members who are having a rough morning. The average American coffee drinker consumes a little more than three cups per day. Nine out of ten older coffee drinkers enjoy a cup with breakfast while only 70 percent of 18-to-24-year-olds do.[1]

74. Brew tea

After water, tea is the second most consumed drink beverage in the world. The four main varieties of tea are black, white, green, and oolong. Quenching people's great thirst for the steeped beverage requires more than three million tons of tea to be produced each year.[2]

75. Calculate a budget

It's true, money talks. The trick is teaching our kids to make their money say hello more often than it says goodbye. Though young teens have limited income, it's no excuse for pushing learning about money management back to a later date. The numbers don't need to be cast in stone, yet teaching them to set a budget from their earnings to fund their savings, spending, and giving accounts is a good habit to start early.

76. Calculate gratuity/tip

Here's a tip about gratuity. For many people working in the service industry, tips account for a substantial part of their income. Where gratuity used to be about customers showing their appreciation for good service, tipping has become a way for many businesses to offset hourly employee wages. Many employers can claim a tip credit, which allows them to pay a subminimum wage, as long as tips bring the total pay up to at least the legal minimum wage.[3] Sound confusing? That's because it can be, especially for people in the service industry working hard to tip the scales of their earning. By teaching your kid to tip well after receiving good service, they can make a real difference in a server's life.

77. Care for their feet

Witnessing your child's first steps is a momentous and memorable experience. Consider this. Those staggering tootles are only the initial few of more than two hundred million strides they will take in a lifetime. It's important not to tiptoe around why your kid needs to care for the over 50 bones, 200 muscles, 60 joints, tendons, and ligaments that will carry them from childhood through adulthood on a walking journey of more than 115,000 miles.

78. Clean inside of car

Results from a study conducted by the car care products industry discovered a connection between how tidy a person keeps their car and how productive they are when they're not driving. Seventy-eight percent of drivers said a clean car helps them feel more put together and confident in their overall appearance. Of the nearly half of all drivers who admit to having food wrappers, expired drinks, and dirty clothes cluttering their ride, one in five don't even know where to begin when it comes to cleaning their cars. This can make friends calling shotgun or pulling into a date's driveway a very awkward moment. So teaching your teen to do a quick cleanup after each drive can help them feel more sure of themselves both socially and emotionally.

79. Clear a clogged sink or tub drain

Sinks and tubs are plunged with a cup plunger. Different than a flanged toilet plunger, a cup plunger is shaped like a shallow cup with a flat bottom. The flat bottom shape of the cup plunger allows it to suction onto the flat bottom of a sink or tub.

80. Clear a clogged toilet

The number one cause of a blocked bowl is toilet paper overload. Clearing a stopped-up chamber works best when using a flanged toilet plunger. The coned shape of the plunger allows more pressure to be directed toward pushing the jam free rather than splashing water and . . . stuff . . . up and out of the bowl.

81. Cook dinner for themselves

Your kid's ability to cook for themselves isn't just about never missing a meal. Good health starts with good food choices. There's nothing wrong with the occasional movie night pizza dinner. Yet easy-to-prep fast food should not be their first and only home-cooked meal option. Whenever possible, they need to focus on preparing portion-appropriate proteins, fresh veggies, whole grains, fruit, and dairy options. Teach them to make every bite count and they will enjoy a healthy body, sustainable energy, fresher breath, clearer skin, and better sleep.

82. Cook meals for others

Teens who eat dinner with their parents regularly develop better relationships with them, do better academically, and are at a lower risk of abusing drugs, drinking, or smoking.[4] Have your teen cook a meal for the family a couple times a month. It will also help them appreciate all the meals they didn't have to prepare!

83. Cook on outdoor grill

Those with good grill skills never lack good friends.

84. Do yardwork with power tools

Gas up the mower, start the edge trimmer, and put on those safety glasses. It's time to do some serious yardwork. Whether your kid is trying to earn a few extra bucks or it's time they contribute to keep the place looking nice, it's a good plan to teach them how to safely and properly use powered yard tools. As the old saying goes, many hands make for light work. So get them a pair of gloves and show them the benefits of a little sweat equity.

85. Drive a nail with a hammer

It may look simple, but the craft of hitting a nail square on the head with a hammer is a lot harder than it looks. Anyone who has swung and missed, swung and bent, or swung and sent a nail tinging off across the room knows all about it. Like any task requiring precision, practice makes better.

141

86. Fix a small hole in the wall

Those new to a dorm, an apartment, or a home rental agreement might be shocked to learn a small hole in the wall can lose your kid their entire security deposit. Anything larger than a usual picture-hanger nail-sized hole can get really expensive, fast. A television wall bracket, a bookshelf mount, or a bike handlebar through the drywall should be properly patched with a little elbow grease and a few bucks. That is, if getting that $500 security deposit back is important.

87. Grocery shop with list

Did you know normal shoppers make 1.6 trips per week to the grocery store and each visit takes on average about 41 minutes?[5] It might not make your trip quicker, but now is a good time to include your tween/teen in creating and shopping from a grocery list. Sticking close to the list will help them not make inspirational buys that bite into an already tight grocery budget. Learning about different brands, products, and where things are in the store takes time, so introduce them to the skill of effectively navigating their way down aisles, reading labels, practicing the art of price comparisons, and checking items off the shopping list.

88. Hang a picture

Depending on the weight of the picture, your kids have options when it comes to hanging that family portrait you gave them as a birthday gift. Kidding about the portrait, serious about them carefully considering their picture-hanging options. Where most lightweight pictures can hang on hardware properly secured in the wall's drywall, heavier pictures may need to be hung on a wall stud. This becomes particularly important when the cost of repairing holes in the wall means forfeiting a dorm or apartment rental damage deposit.

89. Introduce other people casually

Knowing how to make comfortable introductions is a good way to build a reputation as a connector. Connectors are able to keep introductions from feeling like an expectation of friendship. If people hit it off, great. Thanks for the introduction.

90. Introduce other people formally

The art of a formal introduction is all about making a meaningful connection. By sharing a small amount of important information about people, they can initiate a conversation. When appropriate, teach your kids to use people's proper name, personal title, and relevant details about why they are being introduced.

91. Introduce themselves formally

Not everybody needs to know everything, but they need to know enough to make your acquaintance. Giving a confident handshake, making eye contact, speaking their own name clearly, and using good manners are all part of your kid knowing how to introduce themselves.

92. Iron clothes

Wrinkles are the frustrating reality of any wardrobe. Good thing ironing them out is a sure way to let off some steam.

93. Learn CPR and basic first aid

Cardiac arrest claims more lives than colorectal cancer, breast cancer, prostate cancer, influenza, pneumonia, auto accidents, HIV, firearms, and house fires combined.[6] If performed in the first few minutes of cardiac arrest, CPR can double or triple a person's chance of survival.[7]

94. Locate a stud in the wall

Most homes are framed with studs in the walls that are spaced apart sixteen inches on center. The best way to find a stud in the wall is by using a handheld electronic stud finder. The "knock test" is a less accurate and very neighbor-annoying way to locate a stud. The hollow sound you hear when knocking on the wall is the space between studs. A more solid sound suggests you have found the stud framework in the wall. In addition to inches and feet, most tape measures have marks every sixteen inches as well. This can help take the guesswork out of figuring out where the next stud is when your kid is hanging a picture, securing a hanging shelf, or deciding where it's solid enough to nail or screw something into the wall.

95. Make a bank deposit

By digital deposit, ATM, or walking into the bank and filling out a deposit slip, either way the money needs to be in the bank. Learning how each of these methods of making a bank deposit works differently is all part of your kid learning to manage their money responsibly.

96. Manage a bank debit card account

Kids who can learn to manage a bank account with a debit card are on the path to practicing personal financial responsibility. Controlling their spending early will give them valuable insight into what it's like to manage money later in life. Teach your kid to be a good steward of accessing small amounts of money now and they are more likely to be good stewards of much larger amounts to come.

97. Manually open garage door from inside

In the rare occurrence that the power is out in your neighborhood or when the automatic garage door opener motor burns out making its last lift, your teen may still need to get the car out of the garage. Opening the door manually from the inside may be the only way they'll be able to get the car out of the garage to make it to school or work on time.

98. Memorize Social Security number

Pop quiz! What's your Social Security number? What a fun game to play until your kid knows their digits by heart. Only nine numbers long, their Social Security number is the unique identifier assigned to US citizens and some residents to keep track of their income and benefits. In addition, your kid will need to know their Social Security number to open a bank account, obtain a credit card, buy a car, obtain insurance, use on tax returns, apply for a passport, access government benefits, and in some states, apply for a driver's license.[8]

99. Open bank account

It doesn't require a large deposit to open a bank account. What is required to open an individual account, different from a joint account shared with a parent, is for the account holder to be at least 18 years old, possess a government-issued ID, and be able to show required personal information such as their Social Security number.

100. Open the door for another person

Being polite or just passing through, opening the door for another person is a good way to show others kindness, consideration, and respect.

101. Operate power hand tools

Not everyone is good with power tools. Yet knowing how to safely operate them is a must for anyone who picks one up. The priority of any project that includes power tools is safety first. From there, the options are as unlimited as your kid's skills and imagination.

102. Pack travel luggage for themselves

There's packing and then there's packing *right*. Loading luggage with the best selection of clothes, travel-sized toiletries, charger cords, and other trip-specific "stuff" can take time and require making some tough choices about what to take and what gets left at home. To help your teen pack properly, it's time to replace that cute little bag from a few vacations ago with a more mature and adult-size suitcase, carry-on, or day pack. Pick a quality carrier and it will work for them for years to come.

103. Practice time management

Teach your kid time management while having the T.I.M.E. of their life.

Think it. Decide what matters most. Set your priorities.

Ink it. Write things down. Schedules, important details, and goals.

Map it. Make a plan. First do this, then that.

Earn it. Take action. Track progress and get an accountability partner.

Learn more about T.I.M.E. in our *Guiding the Next Great Generation* and *Becoming the Next Great Generation* books.

104. Pump gas

Some states require people to be at least fourteen years old to pump gas. In other states, sixteen. Still others require drivers to remain in their car while an attendant fills the tank. Whatever the age or rules are where you live, it's important to understand how the pump payment system works, about the different grades of fuel, how to fill the tank without spilling, and why it's important to replace the gas cap before departing the station.

105. Purchase a book of stamps

Stamps are seldom purchased one at a time. So where can your kid buy them? Beyond the post office, many grocery stores sell books of stamps at the register.

106. Read a level

There are multiple types of levels. Each serves a different purpose and is widely used by professional tradespeople and DIY homebodies alike. When it comes to the basic leveling needs, a torpedo level is an easy-to-read small tool perfect for general use around the house. Inexpensive, portable, and durable, a torpedo level features horizontal, vertical, and 45-degree vials that come in handy when leveling a picture frame, mirror, or surface that needs to be made as flat as possible.

107. Read a tape measure

Teaching your kid to read a tape measure is a skill they will find handy for the rest of their life. From a fraction of an inch to multiple feet, they will be able to measure a bookshelf to see if it will fit in their room, a couch to determine if it will make it through a doorway, and the square footage of their apartment to see if they want your old bookshelf and couch. Keep in mind that in the United States tape measures are marked out in units according to what is called the United States customary system (USCS) of inches and feet. Yet, some USCS tape measures also include metric units of measurement. Knowing which number you are reading—USCS or metric—makes a big difference. One inch and one centimeter, one yard and one meter, are not the same distance.

> **Helpful Hint:** When reading and writing units of measurement, it's important to know that 1′ = 1 foot and 1″ = 1 inch.

108. Replace printer ink cartridge

"My printer ran out of ink" is the last excuse a teacher or boss wants to hear. Besides, the task of replacing an ink cartridge is quick and easy. One thing it's not is cheap. That's because manufacturers make their profit on the ink and not on the sale of printers. So really the only legitimate excuse your kid could have for not replacing an ink cartridge would be, "Sorry. I'm just a broke teenager who can't afford ink right now."

109. Sew on button

Discovery of a loose or lost button doesn't need to be the end of the world. When your kid knows how to sew on a button, their perfect outfit, work shirt, or comfy shorts needing a little attention can stay secure without much fuss. Compared with a pricey and time-consuming visit to the tailor, their DIY fashion fix will take only a few minutes and cost next to nothing.

110. Shave

Whatever you do, don't tell your kids shaving makes their face or body hair come back thicker, darker, or at a more rapid rate of growth. Because it doesn't. As expected, shaving gives cut follicles a blunt tip. These cut tips may feel more coarse or stubbly and might appear more noticeable while they grow out. But shaving does not stimulate new or more hair growth anywhere on the body.

111. Spot-treat a stain

How annoying. How many times a day do you hear your kid say those exact words? "How annoying." According to research about what we find annoying, staining an outfit lands in the top twenty of all modern-day frustrations.[9] Considering we average four true frustrations a day, which adds up to 1,460 per year and some 87,600 over an adult's lifetime, it's a good thing to show your child that occasionally dealing with a little stain really isn't that big of a deal.

112. Supervise younger siblings

It's not all about age. Maturity matters. Taking into consideration the dynamics between siblings is key to knowing when older kids can watch younger family members. Research presented at the national conference of the American Academy of Pediatrics found that children should be at least twelve years old before being left alone for more than four hours.

113. Take trash and recycling bins to curb for scheduled pickup

It's a weekly thing. Thank goodness. Those bins can get full fast. Looking for a tip for inspiring your kid to remember to take the bins to the curb? Try, "*When* the trash and recycling bins get taken to the curb, *then* you can [*fill in the blank*]," placing ownership of the task in your kid's control.

114. Talk with a person with different beliefs

The key to a good conversation is being a listener. Truly hearing what others are saying is all about paying attention to what is important to them. This doesn't mean your kid has to agree, think, believe, or live in the same way. They don't have to change their mind or convince the other person to change theirs. They do need to respect and value diversity while treating others the way they would like to be treated.

115. Trim fingernails and toenails

If your kid picks or bites their nails, please know they are not alone. Officially characterized as a body-focus repetitive behavior, nail-biting occurs most often during puberty. Around 50 percent of children between the ages of ten and eighteen bite their nails at least occasionally, with boys biting more often than girls after the age of ten.[10] To assist your child in breaking an unhealthy nail-biting habit, help them focus on positive behavior changes or on physical barriers that encourage healthy and attractive-looking nails.

☐ Daily examine, trim, and file nails as needed.

☐ Manicure nails regularly. Kids not wishing to have colored nails can use clear matte coat nail enamel or polish.

☐ Need a little extra aid? Nontoxic bitter-tasting polish is available to remind nail-biters to stop every time they start to nibble.

☐ Stress management techniques like drawing, handwriting, and squeezing a stress ball can help distract from the habit.

116. Turn off sink water lines

When the sound of *drip, drip, drip* is coming from under the sink, will your kid know what to do? Knowing how to turn off the sink's water lines can save money, time, and the need to replace water-damaged cabinets and floors.

117. Turn off toilet water line

Fact or Fiction:

Your kid yelling "STOP, water, STOP!" will keep a clogged toilet from overflowing.

Fiction.

Yes, what they say matters. Yet no matter how many times they yell "Stop," that toilet bowl is going to overflow unless they put their words into action. Teaching your kid how to stop the water from flowing into the toilet before it begins flowing out of the bowl is a skill they hope to never use but inevitably will. When that time comes, you can rest assured, they'll be thankful for your instruction on how turning the valve righty tighty shuts the water flow off.

118. Type on a keyboard

They don't need to type 60 words a minute, but they should know their way around a keyboard. Caps lock, shift, and all forms of punctuation are at their fingertips. Teachers and employers will appreciate their ability to type with more than one finger, and the story they've always wanted to write will come easier if they don't have to hunt and peck.

119. Use an adjustable wrench

Often called a Crescent wrench, the adjustable wrench is one of the most useful tools in any toolkit. Used properly, an adjustable wrench can loosen or tighten most bolts. So be sure to teach your kid the first and most important wrench rule,

Righty tighty, lefty loosey.

120. Wash a car

Keeping a car washed is a low-cost way for kids to protect the value and maintain the appearance of any ride. Dirt, pollen, tree sap, bird poop, bug guts, road treatments, and even air pollutants can damage a car's paint. Regular washing both helps keep a car showing its shine and protects it against the elements that, given enough time, will eventually ruin any car's paint job.

121. Wash and dry clothes independently

Laundry Virgins. Is this subject really appropriate for kids this age? Actually, we debated adding the topic in Stage 2, which would mean kids between the ages of nine and eleven years old might need to know something about what it means to be a laundry virgin. But why, you ask? Because the term comes from one of the most popular television shows of all time that now airs on a network whose programming is aimed at the preteen and adolescent demographic between the ages of eight and sixteen.

Back in 2011, Nick at Night began running episodes of the American sitcom *Friends*. Originally airing weekly on NBC between 1994 and 2004, the show *Friends* was a highly anticipated event for millions of loyal weekly viewers. By the time the series finale aired to an audience of 52.5 million, the show had ignited trends in hairstyles, clothing styles, hand gestures, and catchphrases. One such memorable and well-descript catchphrase was introduced to *Friends* fans in the episode where Ross attempts to teach Rachel how to do her own laundry. While fumbling her way through her first visit to a public laundromat, the twentysomething-year-old Rachel finally admits that she is indeed a "laundry virgin." So relevant and catching is the description, that being a "laundry virgin" becomes an actual thing. And not just as an inside joke between *Friends* viewers from the midnineties, it's still a thing today, thanks to global syndication and programming saturation on channels for kids.

122. Wash dishes by hand

No time to run a cycle? No dishwasher to run a cycle in? No room left in the sink? It's time to rinse, wash, and dry. By hand. A skill as old as eating with anything other than our hands, washing dishes the old-fashioned way will serve your kid well for when they move into their first cheap apartment or get their first restaurant job.

123. Wrap a gift

"Well, it's the thought that counts" is a terrible excuse for a poorly wrapped gift. When presentation is important, knowing how to properly wrap a gift is a beautiful thing.

124. Write a formal invitation

Sure, there's a digital app for that, but there's something special about receiving a formal invitation written on paper. Call it classic, consider it traditional, and even though composing a formal invitation may only come in handy a few times in life, when it does, it really matters.

Just Joking

Kids want the freedom to act like adults, and adults want a snack and a nap.

Teens are like cats. They could probably make it on their own, but someone should probably take care of them.

"When I was a boy of fourteen, my father was so ignorant I could hardly stand to have the old man around. But when I got to be twenty-one, I was astonished at how much the old man had learned in seven years."[11]

—attributed to Mark Twain

Kids would be a lot cooler if every time they shouted, "MOM" or "DAD," it was followed by "You're awesome!" and "Thanks for keeping me alive."

If you are having a bad parenting day and see people staring, they're not judging you. They're just thinking, "Thank you, God, for showing me I'm not the only one who's still figuring this all out."

10. THE LAUNCH LIST—STAGE 4

HIGH, AGES 16–21+

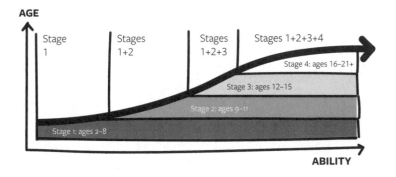

AGE

Stage 1 | Stages 1+2 | Stages 1+2+3 | Stages 1+2+3+4

Stage 4: ages 16–21+

Stage 3: ages 12–15

Stage 2: ages 9–11

Stage 1: ages 2–8

ABILITY

Between the Ages of 16 and 21+ Years Old

Welcome to adulting. Your kids are not all the way there yet, but they are getting closer to adulthood every day.

Soon they will understand why forgetting to take a chicken out of the freezer is so upsetting and how having a favorite burner on the stove is a real thing. It won't be long before they start to appreciate how stuff that used to magically appear in the house, like toilet paper, laundry detergent, and the internet, must be

153

paid for on a regular basis. Just wait, they're about to realize the "life hack" of emptying the dishwasher when it's done so they can skip the step of stacking dirty dishes in the sink *before* loading them into the dishwasher is exactly the same thing you've been telling them to do since they were a kid. Yes, welcome to adulting.

These can be challenging times for your kids. They can legally drive, vote, and maybe even drink. Yet, they are still required to ask a teacher or shift supervisor if they can use the bathroom. Their brains and bodies require more sleep than you, but they often don't start making plans to leave the house till after 10:00. At night! With the power of the internet in the palm of their hand, they can learn about anything from anywhere, yet often struggle to discern fact from fiction. Okay, maybe we share that one in common. Nonetheless, they are just fledglings at this maturity thing, and **believe it or not, they still need you.**

Your kids still need you to be their parent. Some adults are confused about this stage of life and believe it's important to be their kid's friend first, and then their parent second. Truth is, it becomes increasingly difficult to instruct, guide, and council your kid through all they have yet to learn if you put friendship before parenting. This isn't to say raising your kid is supposed to be void of sharing, laughing, excitement, and being there for each other. To the parents who are not also friends with their kids, our hearts hurt for you. What we are saying is, it's important to keep parenting and friendship in the proper order.

The day is coming when you and your kid will agree on many of the same adult kind of stuff. Like, clean sheet day is the best day of the week and figuring out what to make for dinner every night isn't easy. One day they'll quietly sneak out of parties to go home, instead of the other way around. In time they too will complain about how much everything costs. Until then, enjoy them as they are and for who they are becoming.

THE LAUNCH LIST STAGE 4: Ages 16–21+	Skill Level			
Abilities (ages 16–21+)	Not Yet 0	Seen It 1	Can Do 2	Can Teach 3
All abilities in previous stages				
125. Ask for a professional reference				
126. Behave after an auto accident				
127. Behave during a traffic stop				
128. Calculate square footage				
129. Care for leather shoes				
130. Change a flat tire				
131. Change state–issued ID or driver's license to adult status				
132. Check and reset a GFCI electrical outlet				
133. Check and reset a residential circuit breaker				
134. Cook food to safe internal temperatures				
135. Create meal plan for a week				
136. Drink alcohol responsibly (legally)				
137. File annual state and federal tax returns				
138. Fill out a job application				
139. Follow written driving directions				
140. Get driver's license				
141. Interview for a job				
142. Jump-start a dead car battery				
143. Learn methods of protection and birth control				
144. Make living expenses budget				
145. Make personal appointments				
146. Manage a cell phone plan account				
147. Manage a credit card				
148. Manage personal finances				
149. Paint interior walls and trim				
150. Parallel park a car				
151. Pay bills on time				
152. Perform basic automotive upkeep				
153. Practice safe storage of leftovers				
154. Purchase or sell a car				
155. Read and understand terms of rental or lease agreement				
156. Register to vote				

Abilities (ages 16–21+)	Not Yet	Seen It 1	Can Do 2	Can Teach 3
157. Renew driver's license				
158. Renew vehicle's registration				
159. Renew vehicle's safety and emissions inspection				
160. Sharpen kitchen knives				
161. Shift a manual transmission				
162. Stock a pantry				
163. Vote in elections				
164. Work part–time				
165. Work full–time				
166. Write a check				
167. Write a proper email				
Additional abilities:				

"*For those who feel like adults,* most say it's because parents helped prepare them (60 percent), they have a job (60 percent) or they have good role models (49 percent). For those who do not feel like adults, the main reason cited by about eight in ten is because they still rely on their parents."[1]

125. Ask for a professional reference

Some surprises in life are good and some are not. One surprise your kid should never spring on a person is to list them as a reference without first asking their permission. This includes a boss, a coworker, a teacher, a friend, and even you as a parent.

126. Behave after an auto accident

Unfortunately, when it comes to getting in a traffic accident, the chances are pretty good that a fender bender is in your kid's future. That's because drivers in the United States rack up a total of 6 million car accidents each year[2] with licensed US drivers averaging 4 car accidents in the course of their lifetime.[3] Young drivers continue to make the biggest dent in the totals as they maintain the highest rates of car accidents in their first few years of driving. Yet it's important for drivers of all ages to understand that distracted behavior contributes to the cause of over half of all auto accidents.[4]

Keeping the required paperwork about the vehicle's ownership, licensing, insurance, and accident report form all together in the same place in the vehicle is a good practice. Above all else, safety first. Teach your kids that ensuring all parties involved in an accident are physically and emotionally cared for is more important than any assessing of the vehicles' damages.

127. Behave during a traffic stop

Law enforcement makes more than 50,000 traffic stops each day. That's more than 20 million per year.[5] Traffic stop data shows that officers generally pull over Black drivers at higher rates than White drivers and stop Hispanic drivers at similar or lower rates than White drivers.[6]

128. Calculate square footage

How big is this apartment? Will my rug fit in this room? How much paint do I need to buy to refresh the walls in the hall? All good questions that are easy to answer when your kid knows how to calculate square footage and determine the area of a space. Different than volume, square footage is determined by multiplying length by width. Simple math they will remember from grade school once they also remember how to read a tape measure. (See Launch List #107.)

129. Care for leather shoes

A nice pair of leather shoes or boots will set your kid back a few bucks. Learning to polish and protect the leather will keep their investment looking good and wearing well for years to come.

130. Change a flat tire

AAA responds to more than four million calls for flat tire assistance annually.[7] Drivers in the United States rack up over 220 million flat tires per year. That averages out to approximately 7 tire punctures occurring every second. Statistically that means that drivers will experience on average up to 5 flat tires in their lifetime.[8] Remarkably, nearly 60 percent of US drivers lack the knowledge to change a flat tire with confidence. Even more deflating, over 20 percent of drivers admit they are completely "clueless" about knowing how to change a flat tire.[9]

131. Change state-issued ID or driver's license to adult status
Once your kid turns eighteen, they are able to get a new ID or adult status driver's license. The advantage is adult-status issued cards are valid longer than those provided to minors.

132. Check and reset a GFCI electrical outlet
A ground-fault circuit interrupter is an outlet designed to protect people from an electrical shock. Easy to identify, GFCI plugs contain a "test" and "reset" button on the outlet face. Learning when and how to check and reset a tripped GFCI can get a blender, hair dryer, or vacuum going again easily and safely.

133. Check and reset a residential circuit breaker
There are three main reasons why circuit breakers trip.

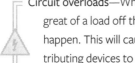

Circuit overloads—When too many electrical devices draw too great of a load off the same circuit, an overload is bound to happen. This will cause the circuit breaker to "trip." Try redistributing devices to other circuits to reduce the electrical load.

Short circuit—When the "hot" wire comes into contact with a "neutral" wire in an electrical device or outlet, a large amount of current flows through the circuit, creating more heat than the circuit can handle, tripping the circuit to prevent overheating and potential fire.

Ground fault surges—When the "hot" wire comes into contact with a "ground" wire in an electrical device or outlet, this causes more electricity to pass through the circuit than the circuit can handle, tripping the circuit to prevent overheating and potential fire.

134. Cook food to safe internal temperatures

The Centers for Disease Control and Prevention estimates that roughly 1 in 6 Americans (or 48 million people) get sick with a foodborne illness each year.[10] To help keep your kid from falling ill after eating undercooked food, teach them about the proper cooked temperatures specific to meat.

TEMPERATURE CHART

Meat		USDA	
		(°C)	(°F)
Beef & Veal (Whole Cuts)		63	145
Minced Beef (Beef Burgers)		72	160
Other Minced Meats & Sausages		74	165
Lamb (Whole Cuts)		63	145
Pork/Ham (Whole Cuts)		63	145
Fish		63	145
Poultry		74	165

*USDA stated temperatures are the minimum safe internal temperature

135. Create meal plan for a week

What! You can't just move Taco Tuesday to Friday. Friday is pizza night. Or is it? Meal planning for the week ahead can be as adventurous as your kid's cravings. To assist them in both creating and organizing a week's menu, consider gifting them a magnetic grocery list pad for the refrigerator. Creating a grocery list *before* heading to the store can help them plan for what to buy and when to prepare specific meals. They'll quickly learn that today's well-planned dinner can be saved for a delicious leftovers lunch tomorrow.

136. Drink alcohol responsibly (legally)

As discussed in chapter 1, one well recognized stage of adulthood arrives when the age of majority, or the age of license, allows for the legal consumption of alcohol. Choosing to drink is a decision that requires responsible judgment prior to any amount of consumption. The best way to

159

guide your kid to make good choices about drinking is to teach them the value of resolving what they will and will not do before acting. This will help them know if they want to partake, when and why it's important to drink responsibly, and to never drink and drive.

137. File annual state and federal tax returns

Whether your child is required to file their own tax return depends on the applicable standard deduction and how much "earned income" and "unearned income" they had during a given tax year.

- Earned income: A dependent child who earns income from working must file a return only if the total of their earning is more than that tax year's standard deduction.
- Unearned income: A dependent child who has unearned income from investments must file a return if the total is greater than that tax year's requirements.

138. Fill out a job application

An application can be a potential employer's first impression of your kid. Help them make a good first impression by teaching them to use good penmanship, answer all questions truthfully, and completely fill out all required information before turning in their application.

139. Follow written driving directions

Digitally dictated driving directions are a modern miracle. As convenient as updated mapping apps can be, they quickly prove useless when directions to the music festival's campsite include, "When you get to the old red barn, turn right off the paved road." Teaching your kid to read road signs, track distances on the car's odometer, and follow written directions may seem old school, but it will sure come in handy when they are out of cell service or trying to find their friend's remote lake cabin.

140. Get driver's license

With so many ride-sharing services and public transportation options, many young people aren't in any hurry to get behind the wheel. Understandable, yet getting a driver's license is about more than the freedom to cruise around. Being able to drive themselves to practice, rehearsal, school, or a friend's frees up parents from having to act as the family's personal chauffeur. Picking up younger siblings, running errands, or helping with the driving are all part of growing up and doing what is needed to help out around the house—or in the car.

141. Interview for a job

In addition to a good handshake, being prepared, and having a teachable attitude, how a person dresses for a job interview makes a strong impression. Your kid knowing that what they wear to work is about putting the company first, ahead of their personal style, is one reason they will have a good chance of acing the interview and landing the job.

142. Jump-start a dead car battery

Shocking news! The paltry 12 volts DC power car batteries deliver won't give your teen much of a jolt if they touch both terminals on a car battery at the same time. Certainly nothing like the electric torture and confession scenes in the movies. That's just bad script writing. What is very real is teaching your teen to NEVER attempt to charge or jump-start a battery that is frozen or low on electrolyte, as the battery may rupture or explode. Electrolyte is the liquid substance found in most car batteries. It is a mixture of sulfuric acid (H_2SO_4) and distilled water.

143. Learn methods of protection and birth control

Your kid doesn't have to be sexually active before needing to know about protecting themselves and others during sexual activity. When considering or engaging in physical intimacy, it's important to understand that methods of protection and birth control are the responsibility of both people. Knowing the differences between protection, birth control, contraception, and contragestion is key to making informed and mature decisions about sex.

◻ Protection: A device used during sex to prevent conception and or the spread of diseases.

- Birth control: Control, and especially limitation, of the number of children born, chiefly through the use of contraceptive techniques.[11]
- Contraception: The prevention of conception or impregnation.[12]
- Contragestion: Any contraceptive method that specifically prevents the gestation of a fertilized egg.[13]

144. Make living expenses budget

Mature kids *Do This*: Set and keep to a personal budget that includes spending, saving, giving, and investing. *Not That*: Using money you haven't earned to buy things you don't need to impress people you don't like.[14]

145. Make personal appointments

Arranging to meet with a teacher during their office hours. Booking a dentist or doctor's appointment. Making dinner reservations. All these personal appointments are just a phone call or online click away and your kid is perfectly capable of making them for themselves. Sure, you may have to coach them through it the first few times. That is, unless you want to be their personal concierge long after they are done with puberty.

146. Manage a cell phone account

Take advantage of those family plan discounts as long as possible. Still, it's never too early to include your kid in reviewing the monthly data plan bill. Nationwide cell service and lightning-fast Wi-Fi are anything but cheap. They need to know just how valuable their access to tech is if they are going to ease into picking a plan that fits their budget one day.

147. Manage a credit card

Teach your kids to own their credit card or their credit card will end up owning your kids. Owing money to a credit card company is like being enslaved to debt. The key to your kids' avoiding the bondage of debt is their not spending what they don't have. Freely spending your money makes matters even worse. Learning to manage expectations, delay gratification, and always pay what they owe will help keep your kids financially free.

148. Manage personal finances

Knowing what money is coming in and where it's going out are the bookends of your kids managing their personal finances. Between the ingress and egress of their money are their financial goals, monitoring, stewardship, and accountability. If you are not the best financial advisor for your kids, find someone who can teach them money management. In the words of one financial wise guy, "If you will live like no one else, later you can live like no one else."[15]

149. Paint interior walls and trim

In preschool your kids were taught how to color inside and hopefully outside the lines too. Now that they are much older, they may need to brush up on their painting skills. Taping off; cutting in; rolling a wall, hall, or ceiling; and touching up trim can both save your kid big bucks and give them the satisfaction of a job well done.

> "Never underestimate the power of a fresh coat of paint."[16]
> Jeremiah Brent

150. Parallel park a car

Fact or Fiction:

Gender influences parallel parking abilities.

Fiction: The fact is, it doesn't matter who is driving. What matters most is your kid's knowledge, practice, and real-world application of angles, depth perception, and spatial relations.

151. Pay bills on time

Paying bills on time is one of the most important things your kids can do to gain and maintain a healthy credit score. Both of the main credit card scoring models, FICO and VantageScore, view payment history as the most influential factor in determining a person's credit score.

152. Perform basic automotive upkeep

They don't have to be a professional mechanic to check the oil, change the windshield wipers and fill the fluid, or add air to a low tire. Basic car upkeep is simple enough that anyone can do it. This means that with a little learning your kid is perfectly capable of keeping their car out of unnecessary trips to the shop to check on the simple stuff.

153. Practice safe storage of leftovers

It's hard to believe how much leftover food we throw away every day. About 68 percent of the extra food we take home from restaurants or don't serve in our kitchens ends up in the trash. That's nearly 80 billion pounds of tossed leftovers each year.[17]

One key to not wasting perfectly good food is to safely store leftovers for later. The highway to the DANGER ZONE for food is found between the temperatures of 40°F and 140°F.[18]

Leftovers left out at room temperature for more than two hours allows bacteria to grow at a rapid rate and become prime breeding grounds for illness. So teach your teen to keep hot food hot and cold food cold and to store leftovers in shallow containers for quick cooling and refrigeration below 40°F within the two-hour time limit.

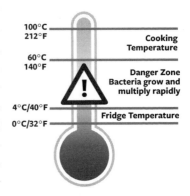

154. Purchase or sell a car

After test-driving, inspecting, and agreeing on a price, there's quite a bit of paperwork that needs to be completed when buying or selling a car. In addition to a sales agreement and legally transferable, properly signed title, your kid may need to complete Odometer Disclosure and Damage Disclosure statements. What forms are required where they live will take some research, but it's well worth the effort. A little online investigating will save them time and a headache when it comes to registering their purchase or sale with the state.

155. Read and understand terms of rental or lease agreement

Month-to-month. A year at a time. Contract deposit. Security deposit. Damage deposit. Grace period. Pet policy. Parking fee. Renewal options. Restrictions. Subletting. Insurance. Early termination fee.

There are so many "fun" terms and "obvious" conditions in a line-dense and legally binding rental/lease agreement. Who has the time to read or truly understanding all the finite details before signing on the dotted line? Well, welcome to adulting, sweetheart. Reviewing all the fine print with your kid may conjure up the emotions of a root canal, but rental/lease agreements are a must-read for anyone responsible enough to live on their own.

> "Do you know the difference between education and experience? Education is when you read the fine print; experience is what you get when you don't."[19]
>
> Pete Seeger, American folk singer and social activist

156. Register to vote

Each state makes its own election and voting rules, including when and how to vote. Assist your kid in checking with your state and local election office to get the most up-to-date and detailed information. This is their first step in registering to vote.

157. Renew driver's license

States have varying driver's license levels and requirements that your kid will need to update as they grow older and more experienced. Temporary. After nines. Minors. Class. Stages. Online renewal. In-person ordering. Tested. Automatic. Transfer. The driver's license renewal requirements for each state are also different, so your kid needs to check with their DMV to learn the requirements well in advance of needing a new license.

158. Renew vehicle's registration

Most vehicles' registration needs to be renewed annually. This may require the vehicle to pass a safety and emissions inspection in addition to the registered owner paying a fee or tax. Even if your kid doesn't own their car, as it is registered in your name, have them complete the inspection and registration steps, minus your signature.

159. Renew vehicle's safety and emissions inspection

Depending on the class and age of their vehicle, your kid may need to have their car inspected prior to renewing the tabs. Usually both the safety and emissions inspections are performed at the same location, during the same visit. Pass and they are good to renew. If the car fails, they will need to get the required repairs done before retesting. The most common causes of a failed safety and emissions inspection are cracked windshield, overdue oil change, check engine light, loose or leaking gas cap, clogged air filter, defective oxygen sensor, faulty injectors, and worn spark plugs.

160. Sharpen kitchen knives

Even the best knives will dull with regular use. Under "normal" conditions, your kid will need to give a fresh edge to their kitchen knives two to three times a year. Electric sharpeners, manual sharpeners, whetstones, and knife sharpening steel are all effective tools to bring a blade's edge back to life. Just watch those fingers. They'll know the knife is sharp when the blade can slice clean down a sheet of paper.

161. Shift a manual transmission

Fewer and fewer vehicles are being produced with three pedals under the driver's feet. The manual transmission is quickly becoming a thing of the past with only about 13 percent of new cars sold today come stick shift equipped. Those that are, tend to be high-end models reserved for drivers who enjoy the feel of driving. So, if your kid dreams of driving a new sporty supercar, or most every classic muscle machine, they had better get themselves some gearbox experience first.

162. Stock a pantry

Cooking is so much easier and fun when the essential ingredients are stocked in the pantry. Consider the pantry a combination of locations. The cupboard, drawers, refrigerator, and freezer. You and your kid probably will not agree on what staples should be in the pantry or where they are to be stored. All that matters is that they make a list of their favorite foods, the ingredients, and how much they want to keep on hand. Then it's all about a trip to the store. Keep in mind that they don't have to stock their pantry in one shopping spree. Over time will do just fine.

163. Vote in elections

Discussing politics can be a tense topic to bring up around your kids. So be sure to broach the subject during a large family holiday celebration dinner when their opinionated uncle is feeling particularly right. Or lead by example and take your kids with you to the polls. Even if they are not yet eligible to vote, walking them through the process is invaluable modeling of how voting is a fundamental right of every adult citizen in a democracy. Instead of telling them who they should cast their ballot for, guide them through the process of weighing the issues, candidates, and conditions in local, state, and national elections. Knowing that voting gives them a personal voice and choice is a powerful lesson to teach your kids and one they too should respect and protect.

164. Work part-time

After school. Weekends. Holidays and vacation breaks. Getting a part-time job is a good way to earn some much-needed money while gaining important entry-level experience. The sense of pride that comes with earning their own money to help pay for their cell phone, clothes, or car is invaluable.

165. Work full-time

Landing that first full-time job is a big deal. A business believes your kid will bring in more value to the company than they expect to take away in pay. A strong work ethic, integrity, and their dedication to excellence will prove the boss made a good hire. Instilling and reinforcing such values in your kid is never an easy task. But it's well worth the effort.

166. Write a check

Who writes checks anymore? Actually, plenty of people and businesses do. In some cases, a check is the only way to pay a bill. Some landlords and

167

many real estate companies prefer checks. Your kid can pay their taxes with a check, and seldom do banks charge a fee for processing a check. Sure, they may seem old school, but the need to know how to write a check isn't a thing of the past yet. You can save that one for your grandkids.

167. Write a proper email

Unlike a casual text message, writing a proper email is a lot like writing a letter. Maybe that's because the first version of what became known as email was invented in 1965, back when paper letters were all the rage. A proper email includes a subject line, a salutation, detailed writing about a specific topic, a conclusion, and signature. Your kid knowing how to compose a proper email is important when communicating with a teacher, an administrator, a coach, a mentor, any legal or medical personnel, and of course their boss.

Just Joking

You know your kids are adulting when they used to have bedtimes but now they tuck you in and go back to whatever they were doing.

You know your kids are adulting when they put an empty cereal box in the trash or recycling instead of back on the shelf.

You know your kids are adulting when they open a carton of eggs and check for cracks before buying.

You know your kids are adulting when they get a job, work all day, and then complain about still not being able to afford to buy whatever they want.

You know your kid is adulting when they say, "I wish the coffee feeling lasted longer."

11. TOOLSET

Following a change of mindset from unwilling to willing, the next easiest way for your child to make the move from Not Ready to Ready is by getting their hands on a good toolset. By *toolset* we literally mean the right tools for the job. Not to oversimply, but when a kid already possesses the *mindset* and *skillset* of Ready, they might only be a toolset gift, borrow, or buy away from assessing an IRL demand as a challenge rather than a threat.

Two Kinds of Tools

There are two types of toolsets, and your child will need to build a collection of both.

The first are the unique instruments needed to perform specific tasks. Like a chef's knife, mechanic's wrench, and a nurse's stethoscope. Each is designed for a particular purpose and rarely can they be used interchangeably. It's next to impossible to slice vegetables with a wrench. A stethoscope will never get a tight grip on a bolt. And under no circumstances should a health exam involve kitchen utensils. It really is important to have the right tool for the job.

The second kind of tool is a little more personal. Not that anyone likes being called a tool, but people are also invaluable instruments—resources with unique strengths. Patient educators, wise mentors, reliable friends, and a supportive family are all essential to your child's current and future success.

With the proper toolset, a willing person is able to put their skillset to good use. Without the right toolset, even the most willing and skilled person may find the simplest of tasks too difficult to complete. Have you ever seen someone try to use a hammer to open a can or seek legal advice from a grocery clerk? And how did that work out for them? Devices, equipment, resources, and access to good people are all important tools needed to get things done effectively and successfully.

One of our favorite examples of how getting ahold of the right tools helped a teenager move from Toolset (−) Not Ready to Toolset (+) Ready happened to a young man we know named Josh. An easy setup for the story might be the old adage "You're only as good as the tools you use." That is, until a kid finds themselves with no tools to use at all, which was exactly the situation Josh found himself in during a very important time in his life.

A Carpenter's Hammer

Looking forward to graduating from high school, Josh knew his next big step in life would not include going to college. Instead, his plans were clearly set on jumping right into a career, and he knew exactly where he wanted to work.

From as far back as Josh could remember, he knew that when he grew up and got a job, he wanted to work with his hands. Indoor office-type work was not the life for him. He was more of a hammer-and-nails, tape-measure-and-saw kind of guy. His calling was clear. Josh had plans to become a union carpenter.

Now that he was graduating and officially a legal adult, his mind was even more made up that he needed to be working outside. "Not that there's anything wrong with working inside, in a cubicle or at a desk," he would say. "That may be the right thing for some people. But it's just not right for me."

We came to know Josh while he was still a student at a leading techical school in Pennington, New Jersey. For his freshman and sophomore years, he attended traditional classes in a traditional high school where he studied math, literature, history, and other required courses. But nothing in Josh's brain or body was excited by learning dictated by bells. He felt bored and held back by the constraints of desks and passive-learning environment of barren classrooms and standardized lectures.

Entering his junior year, Josh moved full-time to a nontraditional technical school in pursuit of a nontraditional career pathway in the trades. Now free to unite working with his hands and mind, his education focused on wrapping up his senior year with not only a high school diploma but also a hard-earned jobsite-ready carpentry certificate.

Well past wanting to get on with his life after high school, Josh looked forward to landing his first real job as a carpenter's apprentice. His lifelong dream of working with his hands was just around the corner. In Josh's mind, the local carpenters' union would mean far more than just a job. It would also provide him with a way out. Out of his broken home. Out of financial hardship. Most of all, he would be free to make the next big step into adulthood as an independent man.

There was just one thing lacking. Much to his frustration, Josh didn't own the tools of the trade. Up to this point, the school had provided all the tools students used to measure, cut, and nail boards into structures. He didn't have the money to buy what he needed, and he knew he couldn't show up on his first jobsite without the toolset required of a carpenter. He desperately wanted to swing a hammer = *Mindset*. He knew how to swing a hammer = *Skillset*. The one thing he lacked was a hammer to swing = *Toolset*.

Following a speaking engagement I had at the technical school, Josh took a chance and asked for help. We sat for a good hour and discussed his situation, timeline, and options. He knew all that he needed was to get his hands on a few of the right tools. Toward the end of our conversation, he politely asked, "Mr. Catherman, do you have any ideas of who I can ask for help?" Unfortunately, at that exact moment I didn't have a name to offer or a solution to his problem.

That weekend I pulled some tools out of my shop in hopes of checking a few fix-it items off my to-do list. Reaching for a saw, for the thousandth time I saw the letters *MO*, engraved on the handle. The initials of the saw's original owner, *MO* reminded me every time I cut a board that when I needed a job to help pay for college, I was gifted the tools I couldn't afford by a master craftsman who believed in me. The toolset MO had given me were all from his own shop, used and clearly well cared for.

Looking around my well-equipped shop, I thought about what MO had done for me so many years before. He helped me with a toolset so I could build a future for myself and my family. Perhaps now it was my turn to return MO's favor, by paying it forward.

The rest of my afternoon was spent packing a crate with as many tools as I could ship to Josh's technical school in New Jersey. He already had the mindset and skillset of a carpenter. Now if all he needed was the toolset of a carpenter, and I owned at least two of almost everything he needed, the right thing to do was obvious. The last tool I packed for Josh was one of my favorite hammers. Just for fun I engraved my initials *JC* on the wooden handle before sealing up the crate and shipping it out.

Josh and I have stayed in contact over the years. After graduation he was hired by his local union as a carpenter's apprentice. His first day on the job, he cinched up his worn toolbelt, reached for his well-used hammer, and got to work. Not only did he look the part, he *was* the part. Just like the other professional carpenters.

Soon after starting his dream career, Josh moved out of his parents' house and into his own place. He saved some money, bought a vehicle better suited for a tradesman, and started to experience what life is really like as an independent adult. Now years later, Josh is a father with two kids of his own. His young adult life doesn't always go as planned, and he's learning to adjust as circumstances change, children grow, and new demands pop up along the way. One thing that hasn't changed is Josh's plan to take on the challenge of designing and building a home for his growing family, with his own hands.

Start Collecting

Walk into any well-equipped kitchen, garage, shop, lab, field house, or maker's space and you'll marvel at the selection of task-specific tools. For every imaginable prep, construct, repair, deconstruct, and innovation situation there's a gizmo, doodad, and thingamajig just waiting to be put to good use by a willing and skilled operator. Such an impressive selection of gear might be a bit excessive for the average person's needs. Instead, an everyday toolset will usually be all your kid needs to start managing life on their own.

Think of the kind of tools most people use on a daily basis. Start with the basic tools like kitchen utensils, cleaning supplies, and time and money management systems. Then there's the need for routine car care and the house, apartment, or dorm room little fix-it projects that need attention before becoming bigger problems. The kind of toolset your kid really should start collecting doesn't have to be expensive or extensive, and it may take some time to acquire. **Add a little skillset know-how, and not only will most everyday tasks be made possible, but a good toolset can also ignite the imagination for what might be possible.**

To help your kid build a basic toolset, we have created a starter list of the must-have kitchen, cleaning, fix-it, car care, and random tools Ready people have on hand and know how to use. As you look over the list, please don't feel the need to rush out and buy everything at once in some kind of tool-time shopping spree. Most of the items on the lists are easy to find, inexpensive, and make a great addition to an already planned birthday, holiday, or graduation gift. However you build the collection, it's good to look for ways to include your child in the process. By actively participating in the collection of their toolset, the value of their hands-on skillset becomes more real and more relevant. As the day of their launch into life on their own nears, both of you can rest assured that, when it comes to taking on life's demands to cook it, clean it, fix it, and drive it, they'll be ready.

12. THE LAUNCH LIST TOOLSET

Fix-It

1. Adjustable wrench
2. Allen wrenches (standard and metric)
3. Broom and dustpan
4. Duct tape
5. Dust mask
6. Ear protection
7. Extension cord
8. First-aid kit
9. Flashlight
10. Glue (standard and wood)
11. Hammer
12. Level (torpedo)
13. Pliers (needle nose and slip joint)
14. Plunger (toilet and sink)
15. Rags
16. Safety glasses
17. Sandpaper (assorted weights)
18. Sandpaper block
19. Scissors
20. Screwdrivers (flat head and Phillips)
21. Socket set (standard and metric)
22. Spray lubricant
23. Steel wool
24. Stud finder
25. Tape measure
26. Toolbox
27. Utility knife
28. Wire cutters
29. Work gloves
30. 1½" putty knife
31. Cordless drill (optional)

Kitchen Utensils

1. Aluminum foil
2. Baking dish (8x8 or 9x13)
3. Baking sheet
4. Baster
5. Blender
6. Bottle opener
7. Bowls
8. Can opener
9. Coffee maker
10. Cutting board
11. Dishes
12. Dish towels
13. Food storage containers
14. Funnel
15. Glasses
16. Hot beverage mugs
17. Hot pads
18. Ice tray
19. Knives (chef's and paring)
20. Measuring cups
21. Measuring spoons
22. Meat thermometer
23. Microwave
24. Mixer or hand blender
25. Mixing bowls
26. Oven mitts
27. Pans (sauté and sauce)
28. Plastic wrap
29. Plates
30. Pots (large, small)
31. Seasoning spices (at least salt and pepper)
32. Scissors
33. Scrubbing brush
34. Serving spoons
35. Silverware
36. Sink sponge
37. Spatulas
38. Strainer
39. Tongs
40. Water pitcher
41. Whisk

Cleaning

1. Broom and dustpan
2. Bucket
3. Carpet/rug stain cleaner
4. Dust cloths
5. Floor cleaner (wood, tile, laminate)
6. Glass/mirror cleaner
7. Laundry basket

8. Mop
9. Rubber gloves
10. Sponges for bathroom cleaning
11. Sponges for kitchen cleaning
12. Toilet brush
13. Toilet cleaning solution
14. Towels (paper, cotton, and microfiber)
15. Tub and tile cleaning solution
16. Vacuum cleaner

Basic Automotive Care

1. Allen wrenches (standard and metric)
2. Emergency blanket
3. First-aid kit
4. Flashlight
5. Jack
6. Jumper cables
7. Lug nut wrench
8. Pliers (needle nose and slip joint)
9. Proof of auto registration and insurance
10. Rags
11. Roadside emergency hazard lights
12. Safety glasses
13. Screwdrivers (flat head and Phillips)
14. Socket set (standard and metric)
15. Spare key
16. Spare tire
17. Tire air pressure gauge
18. Vehicle operation manual
19. Vehicle service log
20. Windshield ice scraper and brush

Random Yet *Important* Tools

1. Backpack/daypack
2. Bank account (checking, savings)
3. Birth certificate
4. Clothes iron
5. Driver's license or state-issued ID
6. External hard drive or cloud storage
7. Health insurance card

8. Luggage
9. Overnight bag
10. Sewing kit

11. Social Security card
12. Umbrella
13. Wristwatch

Important People

1. A few good friends
2. Dorm resident advisor
3. Emergency contacts
4. Faith leader
5. Landlord contact
6. Local elected officials
7. Loving family members

8. Mentors or coaches
9. Personal doctor or health-care provider
10. State-elected officials
11. Trusted confidant
12. Work contacts
13. Work supervisor

PART 3

GO

13. LETTING GO

Looking Back

There are a few daily routines in our home that we really look forward to as a couple. One of our favorites is sitting in view of our garden and easing into the day with some light reading and very dark coffee. About half a cup into the morning, we often scroll through that day's news headlines and a few social media updates. At least once a week, a memories picture pops up on our feed that instantly brings a smile to our faces and takes us back a few years.

There's the photo of when our summer-tan boys were little enough to sit together in a wheelbarrow filled with water from the garden hose. Another of a supportive big brother, Reed, guiding his beyond-thrilled younger brother, Cole, down the backyard slide for the first time. Then there's the image of Cole totally zoned in on assembling a robot at a middle school–sponsored STEAM competition. Another of Reed's puckered face as he bit into his first raw oyster. Pictures like these are blasts from the past and fun reminders of the joy we find in our kids and how we have cherished being their parents over the years. They also cause us to pause and wonder how they got so big so fast. It really does feel like they grew up overnight.

"Cherish every day. They'll be gone before you know it."
How many times did we hear friends and family tell us to slow

down and savor all the little moments with our kids? For sure, it's more than we can remember. Like a sentimental song set on repeat, we now find ourselves singing the same tune to younger parents. But only because it's true. Before you know it, you too will be drinking morning coffee in an unusually quiet and oddly empty home.

Your Days Are Numbered

A friend once sent us a message that read, *"You only get 936 weekends with your kids between when they are born and they turn 18. Make the most of each."* Wow! Stop and think about that for a minute. All added up, 936 weekends to do Saturday-and-Sunday kind of stuff with your kids isn't that many. Sure, 936 is a big number, but considering the demand on our weekend time is usually greater than the supply of hours, 936 weekends doesn't feel like nearly enough.

Maybe that's because the average adult spends more than eighteen hours each weekend taking care of the usual to-do list of life's normal demands.[1] Cleaning the house, grocery shopping, preparing meals, running errands, and trying to squeeze in some much-needed social time with friends. Then there are the far-too-common weekends that require a few unexpected hours at work, maintenance on the car, overdue yard care, a couple extra loads of laundry, and requests to help family and friends with their needs. Dare we mention another travel sports tournament, a return trip to the hardware store, volunteer commitments, club events, church, birthday parties, weddings, maybe some exercise, and please, God, an extra hour or two of sleep. If there's time.

Weekends tend to fly by and Monday arrives with the bang of a starter pistol at the beginning of a race through the week ahead. We're off again, sprinting toward next weekend, doing our best to clear each hurdle along the way. And so the countdown of 936 to 0 weekends with our kids continues.

For those of us who are visual learners, here's what an account of 936 weekends with our kids between birth and their eighteenth birthday looks like.

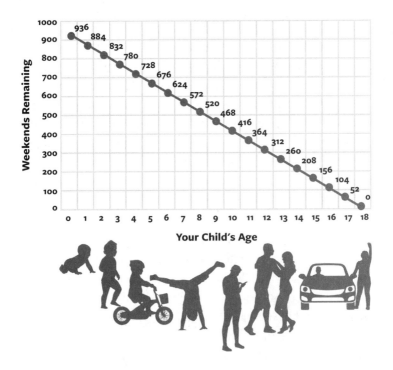

As uncomfortable as letting go often feels, it's an important part of your kid's physical, emotional, social, and cognitive development and maturity. Remember back in chapter 4 when we discussed how helicopter parents often do for their children what their kids could and should be doing for themselves? Again, this is an unhealthy parenting style that restricts kids from the value of practicing levels of independence *before* independence is required of them. Basically, the process of separation from dependency on parents is best done in stages over time. When phased out over years instead of months, weeks, or even days, parents can introduce ways for their kids to experience increased levels of self-reliance with a safety net long before striking out on their own.

Do Bee or Don't Bee Parenting

Are you a Do Bee or Don't Bee kind of person? If this question causes you to tilt your head slightly, curious as to what we are talking about, that's an appropriate response. It's an odd-sounding question to most parents today. But it's one that only a few generations ago set the stage for how many people today are still comfortable receiving instructions on what to do and not to do in life.

To clarify, a Do Bee kind of person represents you on your best behavior, while a Don't Bee implies misbehaving. At least, that's what millions of kids around the world grew up learning while watching the internationally syndicated children's show *Romper Room*. First airing on black-and-white television screens way back in 1953, the show entertained and educated young viewers daily for forty-two seasons. The moral lessons presented in each episode continue to be popular today with viewers of all ages who can now binge-watch the retro episodes online.

For those unfamiliar with the classic television series, imagine a show format that included an oversized bumblebee mascot named Mr. Do Bee and a Do Bee theme song with lyrics about the importance of good manners and childhood safety.

"Do be a sidewalk player. Don't be a street player."

Sounds like familiar safety instructions every caring parent gives their young child.

"Do be a car sitter. Don't be a car stander."

A line obviously written before Click-It-or-Ticket flashed on roadside message signs.

The peppy melody goes on to give kids further guidance on how to live their best life.

"Do be a plate cleaner. Don't be a food fussy."

The song concludes with our favorite line yet,

"Do be a play safe. Don't be a match toucher."

As children inevitably do, the *Romper Room*–watching kids grew up and had kids of their own. And even though we don't have many behavior talks with our children these days that start with "Do Bee" or "Don't Bee" statements, we parents are essentially saying the same thing in our well-intended Do This, Not That life lessons' *teachable moments*.

Have you ever caught yourself thinking or saying, "The way we see it, if kids today actually listened to our Do This, Not That advice, then maybe, just maybe, they would enjoy the good parts and avoid the bad mistakes we experienced growing up"?

Well, maybe, just maybe, it's time we sampled a taste of our own medicine and followed the widely prescribed Do This, Not That advice of family-focused psychologists, therapists, and counselors about how to enjoy one very good and avoid one very bad parenting practice.

Do This 👍
Do be the parent who purposefully releases control of their kids. At the right time.

Not That 👎
Don't be the parent who holds on too tight to their kids. For too long a time.

We offer this bit of professional and commonsense advice in hopes of getting you to think about formulating a plan. A plan that purposefully empowers your kid with time to prepare and opportunities to practice facing the demands of life before they head out on their own. A plan that allows you as a parent plenty of occasions to see your child stretch themselves into healthy levels of independence while they are still living under your roof. A plan that strengthens your bond while simultaneously preparing you for separation.

Essentially, you need a Release Plan.

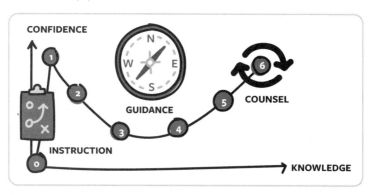

A Release Plan

As final as it may sound, a Release Plan is not about focusing on concluding the countdown of days remaining before your kid leaves home. Instead, a good Release Plan favors time. The more time the better. Your Release Plan should build in as many opportunities as possible for your kid to mature through age- and ability-appropriate transitions from dependent to independent. Transitions made possible by the hands-on and the purposeful parenting practices of teaching by Instruction and release, Guidance and release, Counsel and release.

By providing kids with appropriate Instruction, Guidance, and Counsel, the act of releasing them between each, of no longer exerting control over their decisions and actions, can be carried out over time. This makes the act of a parent "letting go" a recurring cycle that fosters beneficial behaviors and allows your child to practice healthy introductions into independence.

On the other hand, holding on too tight for too long can lead to abrupt cutoffs and last-ditch efforts to put an end to the unhealthy lifestyle of dependency and entitlement.

Get in the Habit

In a way, the acts of letting go or holding on can be considered parenting-style habits. As the formation of both good and bad habits goes, it takes many repetitions to reach a point where you are doing something regularly, without thinking much about it. Such is the case when you parent in ways that create positive teaching and releasing cycles. The same is true for negative routines that create a holding pattern of parental control in a kid's life.

In our local middle school, the student leadership team hung a very powerful poster in the main hallway. As each person in the building, students and adults alike, walks past the sign several times a day, it was the perfect placement for a reminder of where habits come from, how they are formed, and why they hold such significance in shaping one's future.

Watch your *thoughts*, they become *words*.
Watch your *words*, they become *actions*.
Watch your *actions*, they become *habits*.
Watch your *habits*, they become *character*.
Watch your *character*, for it becomes your *destiny*.[2]

Wow! That's quite a progression. What starts off as a simple notion evolves into a pattern and culminates in one's fate. Do you recall the quote by the Roman Stoic philosopher Seneca we cited toward the end of chapter 3? "Let all your efforts be directed to something, let it keep that end in view."[3] With the thought of your kid's best tomorrow in mind, consider how you might answer the following question.

Would you include the words "confident" and "capable" in the description of your kid's destiny? Not as what you *hope* for them in the years to come, but as the result of what you are planning and doing to root genuine self-assurance and true capabilities into their character. Because character will direct their future.

How we impart kindness, confidence, and capabilities to our kids is key to the success of your Release Plan. Getting in the habit of repeating the sequence of Instruction and release, Guidance and release, and Counsel and release creates a healthy pattern of teaching them and releasing them in a way that empowers kids to shed dependence for independence in phases.

Instruction: *I will patiently explain and thoroughly demonstrate for you how to do things.*

Kids are natural-born copycats. They look for parents to set the example and then do their best to replicate the performance. Instruction is all about parents talking the talk and walking the walk in ways that clearly show the Do This, Not That steps required to make something work.

Instructions are usually initiated by the parent and are best received when your kid's knowledge of the subject is low.

and release: Now that they have been instructed on how to do something, give them time to practice doing it. At first they will struggle and probably won't be very good. But with practice and patience, they will get better. Allowing them to work on improving, despite expected difficulties, will strengthen their sense of self-confidence and self-efficacy.

Guidance: *I will provide you with useful information and helpful suggestions, as needed, to further your development.*

When it comes to providing your kid with the guidance they need to resolve, maintain, and advance, it's important to remember that your timing matters. Offered too early, and a parent's well-intended suggestions can come across sounding like instructions. Offered too directly, and a helpful hint may be interpreted as opinionated. Too late, and why bother? Instead, guidance is a well-informed, well-timed, well-presented *option* your kid can add to their developing mindset, skillset, or toolset.

The appeal for guidance can be initiated by either the parent or their kid and is taken best when the kid has a moderate understanding of the subject matter.

and release: Providing your kids with good guidance shouldn't come with the expectation that what you suggest is what they will do. Now that they have some more information, let them decide how and when they will use it.

Counsel: *I will thoughtfully share my best recommendation when you ask for it.*

Counsel works best when it's wanted. You'll know your advice, experience, and wisdom are not only needed but also valued when your kid seeks you out and asks for your counsel. Similar to guidance, the counsel you provide should be based in useful information and helpful suggestions that your kid can take into careful consideration.

The request for counsel is best initiated by your kids and is valued most when their subject-matter knowledge is moderate to high.

and release: Because they care about what you have to say, they asked. At the same time, encourage your kids to seek a second opinion. After all, "the more wise counsel you follow, the better your chances."[4]

In Real Life

Cole was about seven years old when he learned to drive. At least that's what he thinks.

Wanting to go play with a friend, Cole asked if we would drive him over to Mike's house. We were both busy at the time, so we told him he'd have to wait an hour until we were done with work.

"That's okay. I'll just drive myself." He sounded so confident in his abilities, we decided to play along. For a minute.

"You'll drive yourself? And when exactly did you learn how to drive?" we asked.

"Dad taught me. And you said that I'm a very good driver," Cole reminded us.

That's when we realized Cole was convinced that the couple of times he sat on Dad's lap "steering" the car down our quiet lane and into the driveway made him an experienced driver. And Dad's praise of Cole's little hands holding the steering wheel at the proper position of nine and three o'clock gave him the shot of confidence needed to think he knew enough to cruise on over to his friend's house to see if he could play. Obviously, nothing could be further from the truth. Much to Cole's disappointment.

Shift ahead ten years and Cole had another young driver letdown, followed by great success, shortly after purchasing his first car. Cole worked hard, saved his money, and purchased a car now considered a classic—a 1983 Datsun 280zx. With a five-speed manual transmission, mind you. To say his belief in his gear-shifting abilities was revved a bit high would be an understatement. He was convinced driving a real stick shift would be a transferable skill he had already mastered virtually while drifting modded-out street racers in online video games. Instead, his humility took a

190

serious downshift as he repeatedly ground the gears, popped the clutch, and stalled his car just trying to pull out of our driveway. Cole went from certain he knew all there was to know about RPMs and smooth shifting to realizing that gaining a Top Gear status would take some serious practice. Which he did. As the car-crazed parents we are, we're proud to say it only took a few days before Cole was able to start on a hill without rolling back or burning out the clutch.

The false-confidence rise to sudden-reality-check fall Cole experienced as a seven- and seventeen-year-old "driver" is a perfect example of how kids frequently overestimate their knowledge and abilities when they are new to a task. Simultaneously, they often underestimate how much the actual experts know and all the time and effort that went into their learning how to do what they do so very well.

In the world of social psychology, this is called the Dunning-Kruger effect. Because of the simple way the phenomenon explains how the transition from being unskilled and unaware of it, to learning the skills and abilities needed to succeed, the Dunning-Kruger effect makes a fitting foundation to model your three-phase Release Plan upon.

 Phase 1 = Instruction and Release

 Phase 2 = Guidance and Release

 Phase 3 = Counsel and Release

To set you up for parenting success, here's a quick overview of the Dunning-Kruger effect, followed by how the three phases of your Release Plan help both you and your kid see that false confidence, a sudden letdown, and a slow rise to confidence again is not only natural but beneficial.

A Wild Ride: The Dunning-Kruger

Most of us have experienced a very intense and at times nerve-racking tipping point in early phases of learning something new. Like riding a roller coaster, the steep ascent to the first peak is always an exciting climb. Cresting the rise, we are granted a much fuller view of the track ahead, just before abruptly plummeting down toward what feels like certain doom. Such is the gut-dropping response most people experience when they realize they have grossly overestimated their fledgling abilities.

The roller-coaster-like Dunning-Kruger effect models the rise, fall, and gradual rise again of people's self-confidence as their knowledge grows from a beginner learning a new skill to eventually becoming a skilled "expert."

Dunning-Kruger Effect

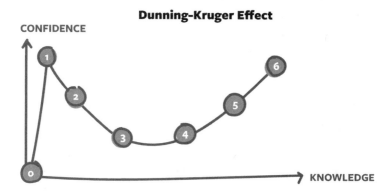

From Point 0 to 1

When people, including your kids, learn something new, it's not uncommon for them to feel overly confident in their beginner-level abilities. This is because even though they only know a little bit about the subject or task at hand, they unknowingly think they know enough. Those who close their mind to additional learning at this point hold a false sense of mastery and often come across as know-it-alls. In fact, they simply don't know that they don't know very much. They are unskilled and unaware of it.

From Point 1 to 2

Those who press on to learn more are quick to realize the actual skillset required for sustainable success is far more complex than they first thought. At this point some kids lose motivation and give up. This is usually the moment when Indulgent parents swoop in, in an attempt to save the day. They'll do anything to keep their kid from feeling the angst of disappointment, agony of defeat, or confusion that accompanies learning they're not the best at everything on their first try. (We discussed the dangers of hovering parents in chapter 4.)

For kids who accept the fact that they still have a lot to learn and choose to press forward, they are in for an unexpected, yet invaluable, additional loss of confidence.

From Point 2 to 3

From the wisdom of the ages comes the saying "The more I learn, the more I realize how much I don't know." Fathoming such a deep truth can be difficult for some kids to comprehend and makes the light at the end of their ignorance tunnel appear dimmer and farther away than it actually is. Hence the definition of ignorance:

ig·no·rance
noun
lack of knowledge or information

From Point 3 to 4

Realizing they don't know much can feel like a real low point for many kids. Their confidence might hit rock bottom, and it can feel impossible to learn what it takes to look like anything other than an idiot. Little do they know, the confidence boost they seek is only a few lessons learned away.

From Point 4 to 5

The more a curious, interested, and determined kid realizes they don't know, the more they want to learn. And the more they discover, practice, and progress, the more they build their confidence. This time the growth in their confidence is gradual and supported by a broader foundation of understanding and relevant experience. They are truly improving.

From Point 5 to 6

Confident in their abilities once again, their command of a skillset becomes fluid. Ever growing, maturing, and open for new or better information, they see learning to master a skill as a lifelong process that requires constant development.

Your Release Plan

Looking back at the Launch List of Skillsets and Toolsets that need to be acquired before heading out on their own, you can't deny the list is pretty extensive. As you rank your kid's skill levels specific to each item, you are essentially assessing their early levels of confidence and knowledge of their abilities. Knowing most children, tweens, teens, or young adults experience the Dunning-Kruger effect while learning how to "master" the abilities needed to take on the challenges of life's many demands, it's important we understand how parents can calibrate their Release Plan to help their kids learn best.

Naturally, kids look to their parents to provide them with the support needed to grow from knowing nothing, to confidently thinking they know it all, to realizing how little they actually understand, to rebuilding their confidence through ongoing learning, practice, and celebrated progress. By syncing the three phases of a Release Plan's Instruction and release, Guidance and release, and Counsel and release with the predictable path of the Dunning-Kruger effect, you can make the most of each time your kid learns to do something new. Let's look at how these function when combined.

Release Plan

![Instruction icon] **Instruction:** As you patiently teach your kids how to do something new, it's likely they will experience a surge in self-
confidence. Oddly enough, their big spike in confidence is fueled
by knowing so little. As soon as they learn a tiny bit, it's easy for
them to think they are experts. Those who stop learning here often
maintain an immature and false belief of "I got this" when looking
through the lens of their beginner-level skills. To help them avoid
stalling out early, try to keep these three strategies in practice as a
parent:

1. **Keep your cool.** "You have no idea" and "Just you wait"
   are far from encouraging statements. Instead, be quick to
   listen for newfound enthusiasm, slow to lecture about all
   they don't know yet, and avoid getting angry about their
   proud, barely amateur status.

2. **Be understanding.** We have all been there, done that. Over-
   assured combined with under-able is like a vigorously
   shaken mixture of oil and water. They take time to separate. Instead of pointing out the inconsistencies in their
   confidence and knowledge levels, try recalling what it's
   like to be excited about something new and let them settle
   into the experience.

3. **Stay the course.** Remember, they are just getting started. The initial steep climb is just the buildup of potential energy.

and release: Encourage them to keep going. To keep learning. There's always more to discover, gather, and understand. But if they're done for now, let it go. Kids who are truly interested will press forward and pick up momentum. If they don't, at least they've learned the basics.

From Point 1 to 2: The Slippery Slope

Guidance: Kids who choose to continue learning quickly see that things are far more involved than they had first believed. If they are going to lose confidence and motivation, this is the time. Now is when parents need to focus on two important things:

1. **Set goals.** Your kid's continued progress hinges on their goals. Setting and achieving goals is all about identifying where they are now (point A) and creating a plan for how they will get to where they want to be (point B) within a measurable duration of time. Goals are not vague, wishful, when-they-get-around-to-it kinds of statements. Specificity is the name of the goals game. Here are a few age-specific examples.

   - (Ages 2–8) "Before my birthday in exactly nine days, I will learn how to tie my shoes all by myself" is a goal. "Wish I could tie my own shoes" is not a goal.
   - (Ages 9–11) "Starting winter semester, I will wake up to an alarm on school days" is a goal. "My parents really want me to start getting up on my own" is not a goal.

- (Ages 12–15) "I will practice guitar for forty-five minutes every day for the next two weeks so I can play along with my cousins on vacation" is a goal. "I want to be a better guitar player" is not a goal.
- (Ages 16–21) "I'll save all the money from my summer job and buy a car I can drive to college next year" is a goal. "It would be great to have a car at college" is not a goal.

2. **Get help.** In addition to your role as a parent, the help of a trusted teacher, a coach, a trainer, a mentor, or an accountability partner can keep your kid engaged and moving forward. The importance of someone assisting them in setting and achieving their goals is huge. How huge? The probability of completing a goal rises from 10 to 95 percent when accountability is included in the pursuit of measurable goals.[5]

Probability of Completing a Goal

10%	If they just have an idea for a goal
25%	If they decide to pursue a goal
40%	If they decide when they will work on a goal
50%	If they create a plan for pursuing a goal
65%	If they commit to someone else that they will work on their goal
95%	If they meet with someone regularly who can hold them accountable to achieving their goal

and release: Seeing little *immediate* improvement in self-confidence and abilities, some parents rush the process and step in to help or protect their kid at this point by helicopter parenting. The bad habit of hanging around and holding on too long can be detrimental to a kid's development of true independence. The truth is, no parent can force their kid to reach their goal and simultaneously retain the value of accomplishing it.

From Point 2 to 3: Question Everything

 Guidance: As the extent of what still needs to be learned is realized, many kids begin to ask themselves "why?"

"Why bother?"

"Why should I even care?"

"Why continue when *obviously* I know *nothing* and it will take forever to learn?"

This is the perfect time to encourage your kid to practice with purpose.

- Introduce them to the truth about practice. Practice does not make perfect. Practice makes better. So when they compare their performance with others who have had more practice, redirect their focus. There's far less value in focusing on the way they best *perform* than there is studying the way they best *practice*. The purpose of practice is to get better.

and release: Now is not the time to bring up the 10,000 Hour Rule.[6] No kid wants their early attempts to learn more to be compared to world-class performers. Yes, concert violinists, Broadway performers, and sponsored gamers commit something like 10,000 hours to practice before reaching the pinnacle of their professional-level success. But we're talking about your kid practicing life skills like politely answering the phone, folding clean laundry, and preparing a meal for themselves. Save the debate over how much practice is needed for true expertise for future grand aspirations, professional pursuits, or potential Olympic aims.

From Point 3 to 4: Not All Doom and Gloom

Guidance: The feeling of "Am I even learning anything?" can be hard to handle for most kids. Helping them see their progress more clearly creates a way to measure their growth. Tracking incremental steps in learning, development, and skills on a progress bar, chart, timetable, or checklist can be simple and a visually encouraging reminder of just how far they have come compared to what still remains.

and release: People progress at different rates and at different intensity levels. Where one kid's confidence may recover quickly as their knowledge and skills increase, another really has to push to keep up. It's important to remember everyone is unique, and seldom are two people encouraged to make progress in the same way. Holding on to what worked for you and expecting the same to benefit your kid could very easily backfire. Instead, find what works for them and do it as often as needed. Find out what doesn't work, and stop doing it.

From Point 4 to 5: Phoenix Rising

Guidance: Everyone likes to celebrate success. As your kid begins to see they are indeed making progress, it's time for some praise. No, not every accomplishment deserves a trophy and not all growth warrants a party. Yet kids need to know that when it comes to gaining knowledge and skills, there is no finish line, so we celebrate the milestones along the way.

and release: How would they have made it this far without your help? It's true that without you the trials would have been greater, tests harder, and struggles longer. Yet the reason you guide them through thick and thin is to demonstrate how they can indeed do this without you. Be pleased. Be proud. **Walk beside them guiding, not behind them pushing.**

From Point 5 to 6: Well Worth It

Counsel: The truth is, maturity seeks counsel. As your kid matures, they will come to you for more than the information your instruction and guidance provide. Ultimately, they are responsible for their own decisions, yet in receiving your counsel, they are requesting to borrow from your lifetime of knowledge, experience, understanding, and sound judgment. They are asking for you to share your wisdom with them.

and release: Steward the occasion well. Share what you can as a trusted advisor and value that they too, just like you, must decide for themselves what thoughts, words, actions, habits, character, and destiny they choose from here.

Déjà Vu

Warning: Riding the Dunning-Kruger effect roller coaster in a way that simultaneously teaches and releases your kid to become more confident and capable often induces the feeling of a visit to the Office of Redundancy Office. But only if you're doing it right.

Just when you've cycled through Instruction and release of this, that, and countless other things with your toddler, it's time to teach them new "big kid" stuff. Thinking you've given all the Guidance and release any one tween can take, they face a situation you don't remember experiencing until you were well into high school. Next thing you know, you're back to white-knuckled Instruction with your teenager on how to parallel park while also attempting to give them Guidance about dating. And they're convinced you don't know a thing about either.

Nobody said teaching our kids to shed the dependence of childhood for the independence of maturity would be easy. It can absolutely be a strain on both you and your kids. Which makes it all the more important that you stay true to your *why* in your dedication to being a good parent. Don't let that inner voice saying "I knew it would be hard, but nobody said it would be this hard" become a dissuader from your commitment to provide the very important Instruction, Guidance, and Counsel your kids need. And Release.

CONCLUSION

In the fall of 2021, our older son, Reed, left for college. Finally. It's not that he had outstayed his welcome in our home. On the contrary, we were sad to see him go. But it was time.

Like so many other young people his age whose plans were put on hold by the COVID-19 pandemic, Reed was forced to delay moving into university housing. Instead of professors, friends, and and new roommates, he stayed home and attended classes online. After a year and a half, he had grown tired of seeing the same faces, and the walls of his "dorm room" over our garage were closing in a little more with each passing day. It was obvious he was both willing and able to start living on his own, but the pandemic's restrictions kept pressing pause on all his preparations and expectations.

During Reed's mandated extended stay, we gave him the nick-name of "the roommate." This came after a long conversation about what we could do to make our far-from-normal pandemic life a bit more tolerable. Reed asked that we treat him less like our son stuck at home and more like the college student he was trying hard to become.

So we decided to let go and stop doing some things we had done while Reed was in high school. We stopped "suggesting" when would be a good time for him to go to bed or to wake up. We quit asking about homework or if he was studying for an upcoming test. And we didn't require him to come down for dinner every night. Instead, we decided to let Reed practice being as independent as he wanted.

All in all, Reed was a good roommate. Like most living arrangements where roomies need to share a kitchen, bathroom, parking, and Wi-Fi, we had to figure out ways to work together to accommodate our differing schedules, needs, and interests. Other than the occasional late-night jam session with friends online, Reed was pretty quiet. Once demand exceeded supply, he'd do his own laundry. He prepared meals, went to work, attended classes online, paid his bills, and kept himself supplied with the basics. All without us having to tell him what, how, or when to do things. In a way, he lived on his own, in our home. He was independent, under our roof. Thankfully, he still liked family movie and pizza nights, helped clean up around the house, and always made himself available for long conversations about the most current social, political, and environmental issues. Which meant our plan to Instruct and release, Guide and release, and Counsel and release helped make the best of a bad pandemic's living situation.

Still, it wouldn't be fair to say the extra time we got with Reed went as planned. Most of what he envisioned for the first couple of years of college got deleted. The eighteen years we dedicated to raising him ready for life on his own turned into twenty. In a very real and unavoidable way, we were once again reminded of the fact that . . .

Raising kids never goes according to plan. Yet, no one should raise kids without one.

It doesn't seem to matter if they are two or twenty-two years old. What our kids need to learn and how we teach them to deal with the demands of life are in a constant state of flux. Those who understand that flexibility is a critical clause in their "parenting with purpose" playbook will make adjustments as needed. Not because they are trying to be trendy, but because it's our responsibility as parents to be relevant.

As in any situation where we want to be better, adjustments to *how* we do things is expected. **What shouldn't change, under any circumstance, is *why* we raise kids ready.**

The proverb "Raise a child up in the ways they should go, and when they are old they will not turn from it"[1] really helped focus our *why* as parents. As our sons grew from small children to mature adults, we held true to the belief that teaching them young to be kind, confident, and capable would help them discover their purpose and live in their greatness.

Yes, we believe our kids are great. Most parents would say the same about theirs too. It's only natural to believe that who our kids are and who they will become is nothing short of amazing. As we said in the introduction and will repeat here in the conclusion.

We know you want the best for your kids. For them to grow up to have a better life than your own. We want the same for ours. This means the privilege and responsibility we share as parents include great stewardship of the few years they are in our care.

They will soon be on their own. This makes our belief that *their greatness tomorrow begins with our guidance today* all the more significant. So let's do what we can to raise them ready.

NOTES

Chapter 1 Adulting

1. Matthew S. Cornick, *Practical Guide to Family Law* (Clifton Park, NY: Delmar, Cengage Learning, 1995), 229.

2. *Civil Code of the Islamic Republic of Iran*, 2007, 14, https://www.wipo.in t/edocs/lexdocs/laws/en/ir/ir009en.pdf; and "Adults before Their Time: Children in Saudi Arabia's Criminal Justice System," *Human Rights Watch*, 20, no. 4(E) (March 2008): 14.

3. "Cambodia," YouthPolicy.org, https://www.youthpolicy.org/factsheets /country/cambodia/; "Cuba," YouthPolicy.org, https://www.youthpolicy.org/fact sheets/country/cuba/; "Kyrgyzstan," YouthPolicy.org, https://www.youthpolicy .org/factsheets/country/kyrgyzstan/; "Decision Makers Guide—DMG47063," National Archives, HM Revenue and Customs, https://webarchive.nationalarchives .gov.uk/20120207202651/http://www.hmrc.gov.uk/manuals/dmgmanual/html /DMG46001/10_0092_DMG47063.htm; and "Vietnamese Lawmakers Vote to Keep Age of Majority at 16," Thanh Nien News, April 5, 2016, http://www.thanhnien news.com/education-youth/vietnamese-lawmakers-vote-to-keep-age-of-majority -at-16-60924.html.

4. Alabama Code: Title 26, Chapter 1, Section 26-1-1; and Nebraska Revised Statute 43-2101, Section 1.

5. "Mississippi Age of Majority Law," USLegal.com, http://minors.uslegal.com /age-of-majority/mississippi-age-of-majority-law/.

6. "Driving Age By State 2021," World Population Review, https://worldpopu lationreview.com/state-rankings/driving-age-by-state.

7. "Voting Age for Primary Elections," National Conference of State Legislatures, June 25, 2021, https://www.ncsl.org/research/elections-and-campaigns/ primaries-voting-age.aspx.

8. "Marriage Laws of the Fifty States, District of Columbia and Puerto Rico," Cornell Law School, Legal Information Institute, https://www.law.cornell.edu /wex/table_marriage.

9. "States That Allow Underage (under 21) Alcohol Consumption," Britannica ProCon.org, updated March 10, 2016, https://drinkingage.procon.org/states-that-allow-underage-under-21-alcohol-consumption/.

10. Jay N. Giedd et al., "Brain Development during Childhood and Adolescence: A Longitudinal MRI Study," *Nature Neuroscience* 2 (1999): 861–63.

11. Elizabeth R. Sowell et al., "In Vivo Evidence for Post-Adolescent Brain Maturation in Frontal and Striatal Regions," *Nature Neuroscience* 2 (1999): 859–61.

12. R. M. Henig, "What Is It about Twentysomethings?" *New York Times* (August 18, 2010), https://www.nytimes.com/2010/08/22/magazine/22Adulthood-t.html?pagewanted=all.

Chapter 2 Ready or Not

1. Gregory Titelman, *Random House Dictionary of Popular Proverbs and Sayings* (New York: Random House, 1996).

2. Jim Blascovich, "Challenge and Threat," in *Handbook of Approach and Avoidance Motivation,* ed. A. J. Elliot (New York: Psychology Press, 2008), 431–45; and Jim Blascovich and Wendy Berry Mendes, "Social Psychophysiology and Embodiment" in *Handbook of Social Psychology*, 5th ed., ed. Susan T. Fiske et al. (New York: Wiley, 2010).

Chapter 3 The Readiness Assessment

1. Des Bieler, "Kid Comes Out of the Stands and Takes a Point Off of Roger Federer," *Washington Post*, March 12, 2015, https://www.washingtonpost.com/news/early-lead/wp/2015/03/12/kid-comes-out-of-the-stands-and-takes-a-point-off-of-roger-federer/.

2. Lucius Annaeus Seneca, *Hardship and Happiness (The Complete Works of Lucius Annaeus Seneca)*, trans. Elaine Fantham, Harry M. Hine, James Ker, and Gareth D. Williams (Chicago: University of Chicago Press, 2014).

Chapter 4 Mindset

1. Gabriel Lopez-Garrido, "Self-efficacy," Simply Psychology, August 9, 2020, https://www.simplypsychology.org/self-efficacy.html.

2. Albert Bandura, *Self-Efficacy: The Exercise of Control* (New York: W. H. Freeman, 1997).

3. John Medina, *Brain Rules: 12 Principles for Surviving and Thriving at Work, Home, and School* (Seattle: Pear Press, 2008), 60.

4. Tom Harpole, "Falling with the Falcon," *Air & Space Magazine*, March 2005, https://www.airspacemag.com/flight-today/falling-with-the-falcon-7491768/.

5. Jennifer Mangaly, "How Do Penguins Move?" Sciencing, updated November 22, 2019, https://sciencing.com/penguins-move-4567706.html.

6. "New 911 GT2 with 530 Horsepower," New Press Release, Porsche, July 16, 2007, https://www.porsche.com/usa/aboutporsche/pressreleases/pag/?pool=international-de&id=2007-07-16.

7. "Carbon Arrow Basics and Measurement Standards, Chapter 1," Hunter's Friend, https://www.huntersfriend.com/carbon-arrow-basics-measurement-standards-research-guide.html.

8. Efstathios D. Gennatas et al., "Age-Related Effects and Sex Differences in Gray Matter Density, Volume, Mass, and Cortical Thickness from Childhood to Young Adulthood," *Journal of Neuroscience* 37, no. 20 (May 17, 2017): 5065–73, https://www.jneurosci.org/content/37/20/5065.

9. University of Michigan. "Failure to Launch: Parents Are Barriers to Teen Independence," ScienceDaily, July 22, 2019, www.sciencedaily.com/releases /2019/07/190722085830.htm.

10. Georgetown University Center on Education and the Workforce, *Born to Win, Schooled to Lose: Why Equally Talented Students Don't Get Equal Chances to Be All They Can Be*, 2019, https://cew.georgetown.edu/cew-reports /schooled2lose/.

11. Richard S. Lazarus, "How emotions influence performance in sportsy," *Sports Psychologist* 14, no. 3 (2000): 229–52, https://doi.org/10.1123/tsp.14.3.229.

12. Richard S. Lazarus, *Psychological Stress and the Coping Process* (New York: McGraw-Hill, 1996).

13. Diana Baumrind, "The Influence of Parenting Style on Adolescent Competence and Substance Use," *Journal of Early Adolescence* 11, no. 1: 56–95, https:// doi.org/10.1177/0272431691111004.

14. Diana Baumrind and Allen E. Black, "Socialization Practices Associated with Dimensions of Competence in Preschool Boys and Girls," *Child Development* 38, no. 2 (1967): 291–327, https://doi.org/10.2307/1127295.

15. E. L. Deci, H. Eghrari, B. C. Patrick, and D. R. Leone. "Facilitating internalization: The self-determination perspective," *Journal of Personality* 62 (1994): 119–42; and M. Vansteenkiste, J. Simons, W. Lens, K. M. Sheldon, and E. L. Deci, "Motivating learning, performance, and persistence: The synergistic role of intrinsic goals and autonomy-support," *Journal of Personality and Social Psychology* 87 (2004): 246–60.

16. Erlanger A. Turner, Megan Chandler, and Robert W. Heffer, "The Influence of Parenting Styles, Achievement Motivation, and Self-Efficacy on Academic Performance in College Students," *Journal of College Student Development* 50 no. 3 (2009): 337–46, Project MUSE, doi:10.1353/csd.0.0073.

17. Charles Ganaprakasam, Kavitha S. Davaidass, and Sivan C. Muniandy, "Helicopter Parenting and Psychological Consequences among Adolescents," *International Journal of Scientific and Research Publications* 8 no. 60 (June 2018): 378–82, http://dx.doi.org/10.29322/IJSRP.8.6.2018.p7849.

18. Foster Cline and Jim Fay, *Parenting with Love and Logic: Teaching Children Responsibility* (Colorado Springs: Pinon Press, 1990).

19. Deepika Srivastav and M.N. Lal Mathur, "Helicopter Parenting and Adolescent Development: From the Perspective of Mental Health," IntechOpen, October 5, 2020, DOI: 10.5772/intechopen.93155.

20. Chris Segrin et al., "Parent and child traits associated with overparenting," *Journal of Social and Clinical Psychology* 32 no. 6 (2013): 569–95, https://doi .org/10.1521/jscp.2013.32.6.569.

21. Jordana K. Bayer, Ann V. Sanson, and Sheryl A. Hemphill, "Parent Influences on Early Childhood Internalizing Difficulties," *Journal of Applied Developmental Psychology* 27 no. 6 (2006): 542–59, https://doi.org/10.1016/j.app dev.2006.08.002.

22. Terri LeMoyne and Tom Buchanan, "Does 'Hovering' Matter? Helicopter Parenting and Its Effect on Well-Being," *Sociological Spectrum* 31 no. 4 (2011): 399–418, https://doi.org/10.1080/02732173.2011.574038.

Chapter 5 Skillset

1. Admiral William H. McRaven, "This One Simple Secret Will Completely Change Your Life Today!" YouTube, https://www.youtube.com/watch?v=3sK3 wJAxGfs&t=3s.
2. *The Alcalde*, Texas Exes, June 24, 2011, retrieved December 17, 2020.
3. "Adm. McRaven Urges Graduates to Find Courage to Change the World," UT News, May 16, 2014, https://news.utexas.edu/2014/05/16/mcraven-urges -graduates-to-find-courage-to-change-the-world/.
4. Jennifer Breheny Wallace, "Why Children Need Chores," *Wall Street Journal*, March 13, 2015, https://www.wsj.com/articles/why-children-need-chores -1426262655.
5. George E. Vaillan, Charles C. McArthur, and Arlie Bock, "Grant Study of Adult Development, 1938–2000," Harvard Dataverse, V4, 2010, https://doi .org/10.7910/DVN/48WRX9.
6. Ami Albernaz, "Sparing Chores Spoils Children and Their Future Selves, Study Says," *Boston Globe*, December 8, 2015, https://www.bostonglobe.com.
7. US Census Bureau and US Bureau of Labor Statistics, Current Population Survey (IPUMS), US Department of Labor, and O*NET, "Share of Under-employed Graduates in Good Non-College and Low-Wage Jobs," https://www .newyorkfed.org/research/college-labor-market/college-labor-market_under employment_jobtypes.html.
8. Hart Research Associates, *Falling Short? College Learning and Career Success* (Washington, DC: Association of American Colleges and Universities, 2015).
9. Charles Kivunja, "Teaching Students to Learn and to Work Well with 21st Century Skills," *International Journal of Higher Education* 4 no. 1 (2015): 1–11.

Chapter 6 Phases and Stages

1. *A Christmas Story*, directed by Bob Clark (Beverly Hills, CA: Metro-Goldwyn-Mayer, 2008).
2. George Kuh, Ken O'Donnell, and Carol Geary Schneider, "HIPs at Ten," *Change: The Magazine of Higher Learning* 49, no. 5 (Nov. 2017): 8–16, https:// www.tandfonline.com/doi/abs/10.1080/00091383.2017.1366805.

Chapter 7 The Launch List—Stage 1

1. UC Davis Center, "Children Learn through Play," www.ucdmc.ucdavis.edu /cancer.
2. National Center for Emerging and Zoonotic Infectious Diseases (NCEZID), Centers for Disease Control and Prevention, accessed February 23, 2021.
3. "Do I Need to Wash This?" American Cleaning Institute, https://www .cleaninginstitute.org/cleaning-tips/clothes/laundry-basics/do-i-need-wash.

4. Kelsey Lynch, "6 Reasons Learning to Swim Can Be Highly Useful," *Swimming World*, July 5, 2020, https://www.swimmingworldmagazine.com/news/6-reasons-learning-to-swim-can-be-highly-useful/.

5. Jayne A. Fulkerson et al., "A Review of Associations between Family or Shared Meal Frequency and Dietary and Weight Status Outcomes across the Lifespan," *Journal of Nutrition Education and Behavior* 46, no. 1 (Jan. 2014): 2–19, http://dx.doi.org/10.1016/j.jneb.2013.07.012.

6. Susanne Kerner, Cynthia Chou, and Morten Warmind, eds., *Commensality: From Everyday Food to Feast* (London: Bloomsbury Academic, 2015).

Chapter 9 The Launch List—Stage 3

1. The National Coffee Association, National Coffee Data Trends (NCDT) Report, March 26, 2020, https://www.ncausa.org/Newsroom/NCA-releases-Atlas-of-American-Coffee.

2. "100 Facts About Tea—The Ultimate List of Tea Facts!" Tea How, https://teahow.com/100-facts-about-tea/.

3. US Department of Labor, "Tips," https://www.dol.gov/general/topic/wages/wagestips.

4. "The Importance of Family Dinners VIII," A CASAColumbia White Paper, National Center on Addiction and Substance Abuse at Columbia University, September 2012.

5. FMI US Grocery Shopper Trends, 2018; US Bureau of Labor Statistics, CEX, calculations by The Hartman Group.

6. Centers for Disease Control and Prevention, National Vital Statistics Reports, December 29, 2011, http://www.cdc.gov/nchs/data/nvsr/nvsr60/nvsr60_03.pdf.

7. CPR Facts and Stats, CPR and First Aid, https://cpr.heart.org/en/resources/cpr-facts-and-stats.

8. State of California Department of Motor Vehicles, "Social Security Number," https://www.dmv.ca.gov/portal/driver-education-and-safety/educational-materials/fast-facts/social-security-number-ffdl-8/; and New York State Department of Motor Vehicles, "How to apply for a 'Standard' License without a Social Security Number or Ineligibility Letter," https://dmv.ny.gov/driver-license/applying-standard-license-without-social-security-number-or-ineligibility-letter.

9. Survey conducted by OnePoll, with a sample of 2000 US residents in 2016.

10. Healthwise Staff, "Nail-Biting," C.S. Mott Children's Hospital, July 2, 2020, https://www.mottchildren.org/health-library/tw9722spec.

11. Fred R. Shapior, *The Yale Book of Quotations*, New Haven: Yale University Press, 2006.

Chapter 10 The Launch List—Stage 4

1. *Young Americans and Money*, Bank of America/USA TODAY Better Money Habits Report, Fall 2016, 3, https://about.bankofamerica.com/assets/pdf/BOA_BMH_2016-REPORT-v5.pdf.

2. "Car Accident Statistics in the US," Driver Knowledge, https://www.driverknowledge.com/car-accident-statistics/.

3. Des Toups, "How Many Times Will You Crash Your Car?" https://www
.forbes.com/sites/moneybuilder/2011/07/27/how-many-times-will-you-crash
-your-car/?sh=417eaf4e6217.

4. "Using Naturalistic Driving Data to Examine Teen Driver Behaviors Present
in Motor Vehicle Crashes, 2007-2015," AAA Foundation for Traffic Safety, June
2016, https://aaafoundation.org/using-naturalistic-driving-data-examine-teen
-driver-behaviors-present-motor-vehicle-crashes-2007-2015/.

5. Frank R. Baumgartner, Derek A. Epp, and Kelsey Shoub, *Suspect Citizens:
What 20 Million Traffic Stops Tell Us about Policing and Race* (New York: Cam-
bridge University Press, 2018).

6. Emma Pierson et al., "A Large-Scale Analysis of Racial Disparities in Police
Stops across the United States," Nature Human Behavior 4 (July 2020): 736–45,
https://5harad.com/papers/100M-stops.pdf.

7. AAA Newsroom, https://newsroom.aaa.com/tag/flat-tire/.

8. "Tire Repair Kit Facts," Active Tools, http://www.activetools.com/education
-center/the-science-behind-our-compressors.

9. "A Quarter of Americans Are Clueless about How to Change a Flat Tire,"
Town Fair Tire, January 22, 2020, https://www.townfairtire.com/blog/a-quarter-of
-americans-are-clueless-about-how-to-change-a-flat-tire.html.

10. "Burden of Foodborne Illness: Findings," National Center for Emerging
and Zoonotic Infectious Diseases (NCEZID), Division of Foodborne, Water-
borne, and Environmental Diseases (DFWED), https://www.cdc.gov/foodborne
burden/2011-foodborne-estimates.html.

11. *American Heritage Medical Dictionary*, s.v. "birth control," retrieved
August 9, 2021, https://medical-dictionary.thefreedictionary.com/birth+control.

12. *McGraw-Hill Concise Dictionary of Modern Medicine*, s.v. "contraception," retrieved August 9, 2021, https://medical-dictionary.thefreedictionary.co
/contraception.

13. *McGraw-Hill Concise Dictionary of Modern Medicine*, s.v. "contragestion," retrieved August 9, 2021, https://medical-dictionary.thefreedictionary.com
/contragestion.

14. Robert Quillen, "Paragraphs," *Detroit Free Press*, June 4, 1928.

15. Dave Ramsey, *Total Money Makeover: Classic Edition: A Proven Plan for
Financial Fitness* (Nashville: Nelson Books, 2013), 5.

16. Jeremiah Brent, "Hancock Park Estate," Newsletter, JeremiahBrent.com,
https://www.jeremiahbrent.com/design-firm-portfolio/hudson.

17. United States Environmental Protection Agency, "Sustainable Management
of Food Basics" (2019), EPA.gov, https://www.epa.gov/sustainable-management
-food/sustainable-management-food-basics.

18. US Department of Agriculture, Food Safety and Inspection Service, "'Danger Zone' (40°F–140°F)," https://www.fsis.usda.gov/food-safety/safe-food-hand
ling-and-preparation/food-safety-basics/danger-zone-40f-140f.

19. Valerie Strauss, "Pete Seeger: 'Do You Know the Difference between Education and Experience?'" *Washington Post*, January 28, 2014, https://www.washing
tonpost.com/news/answer-sheet/wp/2014/01/28/pete-seeger-do-you-know-the
-difference-between-education-and-experience/.

Chapter 13 Letting Go

1. Bureau of Labor Statistics, American Time Use Survey, Table A-2A, www.bls.gov/tus/a2_2016.pdf.

2. Generally attributed to Fank Outlaw.

3. Seneca, *Hardship and Happiness*.

4. Proverbs 11:14 MSG.

5. Barrett Whissman, "An Accountability Partner Makes You Vastly More Likely to Succeed," *Entrepreneur*, March 20, 2018, https://www.entrepreneur.com/article/310062.

6. Malcolm Gladwell, *Outliers: The Story of Success* (New York: Little, Brown and Co., 2008), 38–39.

Conclusion

1. Proverbs 22:6, author paraphrase.

Jonathan Catherman is a sociologist and educator who has worked in private and public education for twenty-five years. He speaks worldwide to diverse audiences of all ages and is the best-selling author of *The Manual to Manhood* and *The Manual to Middle School*. For his success in the development and delivery of youth mentoring resources and programming, Jonathan was awarded the President's Volunteer Service Award and Martin Luther King Drum Major for Service Award.

Erica Catherman has spent more than twenty years working with young women as a community volunteer, an advocate for gender equality in sports, and a coach/mentor to middle school, high school, and college students. She has written resources for young women and their mentors and is the author (with Jonathan) of *The Girls' Guide to Conquering Life* and *The Girls' Guide to Conquering Middle School*.

CONNECT WITH

JONATHAN & ERICA CATHERMAN

Authors, Speakers, Consultants, Creators

To learn more and connect with the Cathermans, visit

WWW.THECATHERMANS.COM